THE
VANISHING
PAST

THE
VANISHING
PAST

Making the Case for the
Future of History

TRILBY KENT

**SUTHERLAND
HOUSE**

TORONTO, 2022

Sutherland House
416 Moore Ave., Suite 205
Toronto, ON M4G 1C9

First edition, October 2022

If you are interested in inviting one of our authors to a live event or
media appearance, please contact sranasinghe@sutherlandhousebooks.com
and visit our website at sutherlandhousebooks.com for more
information about our authors and their schedules.

Manufactured in China
Cover designed by Lena Yang
Book composed by Karl Hunt

Library and Archives Canada Cataloguing in Publication
Title: The vanishing past : making the case for the future of history /
Trilby Kent.
Names: Kent, Trilby, 1982- author.
Identifiers: Canadiana 20220226725 | ISBN 9781989555798 (hardcover)
Subjects: LCSH: History—Study and teaching.
Classification: LCC D16.2 .K46 2022 | DDC 907.1—dc23

ISBN 978-1-989555-79-8

For Clea and Tristan

Contents

INTRODUCTION

THIS BOOK GREW OUT of a conversation that took place in a midtown Toronto bar in December 2019. Over the weeks that followed, while I drafted the proposal for a "manifesto" defending the value of historical education, reports began to filter through our smartphones and television screens of a mysterious virus that was claiming an alarming number of lives on the other side of the globe. Parts of China were being shut down in a way that only seemed possible in one of the world's most tightly controlled societies. Images of empty streets and families holed up for weeks in their apartment blocks intrigued and alarmed us. Still, life went on, and for a time these reports were absorbed into a news cycle that included devastating Australian bushfires, a passenger plane being shot down over Iran, and Donald Trump's ongoing debasement of the American presidency.

The proposal was accepted; I signed a contract and started work in earnest. Then, almost overnight, the lockdowns began and life ceased to be normal. To put it mildly, 2020 was an interesting year to spend researching a book on the value of history. Before long, there was talk everywhere of what it was like to find ourselves living through an historical moment, not to mention heightened appreciation for what past societies endured. Some comparisons (of our quarantine experience to Boccaccio's and Defoe's accounts of other plagues) were telling, while others (equating modern-day medics to the soldiers who stormed the Normandy beaches on D-Day) perhaps missed the mark slightly. Prime Minister Justin Trudeau went so far as to call the pandemic "the greatest health care crisis in our history," a rhetorical flourish that ignored the vast range of devastating diseases that humanity has grappled with over time. There was also an element of disbelief not dissimilar to what many experienced observing 9/11 unfold: one of the most popular fallback descriptions of that day was that it was like watching scenes from a disaster movie, a reminder not only of how insulated we'd become against historic calamity, but how arrogant to assume that we'd somehow moved beyond it. Crucially, we now seemed to realize that history isn't inevitable and, more importantly, that we don't exist outside of it.

Next came the questions about what kind of world we wanted to live in after the pandemic, which was clearly going to have a devastating effect on many communities and industries. As far as history was concerned, the UN predicted that one in eight museums worldwide would close permanently, with one in three American museums never to reopen. Collections focused on the lives of Black, Indigenous, and minority groups would be particularly vulnerable. More pressingly, the pandemic was revealing real, life-costing inequities between our living citizens: rich and poor, Black and white.

The sad fact is that we were in trouble long before Covid-19 came along. The killing of George Floyd in May 2020 highlighted once again the problem of systemic racism in America–a problem which also exists in Canada, as the deaths of Joyce Echaquan, Chantel Moore, and others have illustrated– and unleashed a global wave of support for Black Lives Matter. Around the same time, discussions of the legacy of colonialism, slavery, and institutionalized racism provided fresh impetus for such movements as #RhodesMustFall, resulting in a rush of statue-toppling from Montreal to Bristol to Antwerp, and across the United States.

We look to history to learn how to face moments such as these and to remind ourselves that we're a resilient, if destructive, species. War, pestilence and social upheaval have brought numerous civilizations to their knees, but we can also find in history examples of leadership, self-sacrifice, ingenuity, and magnanimity. In the words of Winston Churchill, "the future is unknowable, but the past should give us hope."[1]

It's not just about feeling good, though: the past can and should help inform our actions as individuals and states. Writing in *Prospect* in May 2020, leading historian Anthony

Seldon argued that "[e]very Whitehall department, including No. 10, should have an active historian advising ministers on historical precedent."[2] Such advice, said Seldon, may well have helped avoid the calamities of both Brexit and Covid-19. Some university departments are already on to this: King's College, London has created a Centre for Grand Strategy, which, according to its website, "seeks to bring a greater degree of historical and strategic expertise to statecraft, diplomacy and foreign policy . . . bringing top-class academic expertise to bear on the policy-making process and the public debate about foreign policy." Applied history has also made inroads at Harvard, where the Belfer Center's Applied History Project aims to address the "history deficit" (Niall Ferguson's phrase) in policymaking.

But none of this can happen without a historically literate citizenry. That relies to some extent on flourishing university history departments, and those can't exist without a coherent and wide-ranging history program in our high schools. None of this is likely without our youngest students being introduced to great human stories from earliest times.

When schools shut down in March 2020, the Toronto District School Board sent parents an anaemic list of online education links to keep students occupied while it figured out the practicalities of remote learning. The links focused exclusively on literacy and math, which we've long been conditioned to believe are the two most important subjects our elementary students need to master. What was missing from this list–what, it strikes me, has long been missing from our schools–was the far greater power of *story* to reassure, entertain, inspire, and help students (and their parents) make sense of the strange new world in which we find ourselves.

Stories occupy a deep and powerful position in the human psyche; there's a reason that Einstein advised that parents wishing to raise intelligent children should read their progeny fairy tales and yet more fairy tales. All cultures, even those without written language, share stories. Storytelling was the original form of teaching, which has helped to define communities since earliest times (tempting though it is to argue that the very word "history" is built around "story," it's worth noting that the word actually derives from the Greek *histōr*, meaning a learned or wise man). Today, we know that sharing stories with our youngest students has multiple benefits: growing wonder, curiosity, understanding, empathy, problem solving, and interpretation skills; developing memory; inspiring discussion and debate; nurturing a sense of community; building engagement with learning; and helping young minds organize and relate experiences, and understand cause and effect.

Oh, yes—they seem to help with literacy skills, too.

Of course, you need to learn a lot of stories for all of this to work, and you certainly shouldn't be hearing the same story again and again. Anyone who's watched Nigerian writer Chimamanda Ngozi Adichie's excellent 2009 TED Talk, "The Danger of a Single Story,"[3] will be familiar with the idea that the single story leads to an incomplete understanding of other perspectives and can all too quickly become the *only* story. In other words, as Adichie suggests, a single story of Africa becomes "a single story of catastrophe," robbing individuals of their dignity and emphasizing how we're different rather than how we're similar. Politicians use the single story all the time, as do proponents of orthodoxies on both the Left and Right. Living, as we do, in an era of polarized debate makes it even harder for us to recognize and hear a plenitude of stories.

But this is exactly what we need right now, more than ever: a sense of our place in the great human story, as well as the beautiful, bewildering complexity of the many overlapping stories from the dawn of time to the present day that make us who we are and shape who we will become.

* * *

A disclaimer: I am not a professional historian or curriculum designer. I read modern history as an undergraduate at Oxford, where my course topics ranged from the writings of St. Augustine to the 1968 international uprisings. Undergraduate historians at Oxford study history and nothing but history through a combination of reading, essay writing, lectures and, increasingly, group seminars (when I was there, seminars only took place as part of my special subject in the Indian independence movement and my further subject in the decline of the Byzantine Empire and rise of Islam). In my first week, I was asked to write an essay explaining the "glory" of the Glorious Revolution (also known as the 1688 deposition of James II and replacement by his daughter Mary II and her husband, the Dutch William III of Orange), a topic about which I knew next to nothing. Armed with a reading list and lecture schedule, I had five days to come up with something in advance of my first tutorial (a meeting with my college tutor and one other student) where we would discuss what I had written. From here on, every week followed this pattern. It was, to say the least, a challenging, exhilarating, and immensely rewarding way to learn.

I went on to postgraduate studies in social anthropology at the London School of Economics, before trading academe for journalism and fiction writing. Journalism, it is often said, is the first draft of history, and I had grown up in a family of print and broadcast journalists. We'd moved every few years while my father worked as a war correspondent reporting mainly from South America and Eastern Europe; he'd previously done stints in Africa and southeast Asia. The titles on the spines that filled the bookshelves in our family room spoke of far-away places and conflicts (*Arab and Jew*, *The Boer War*, *Gorbachev*), and I was always eager to receive new souvenirs: a set of matryoshka dolls, perhaps, or hand-painted pan pipes. For years, I imagined that the beaded Zulu wedding apron that hung in our hallway was a giant's glove.

It is safe to say that my taste for story was one enriched with a curiosity about the world beyond my own immediate experience, and this included the worlds of the past. The ancient Middle East, revolutionary Europe, Africa in the dying days of colonialism—these were the places and periods that captured my imagination. Watching my eight-year-old daughter get hooked on the historical role-playing game *Mission U.S.* during the long, housebound days of the early pandemic reminded me of the hours I spent at the same age playing *Oregon Trail* (alternately trying to shepherd my family to the Willamette Valley in one piece and trying to see how quickly I could make them succumb to cholera, typhus, or snakebite along the way). Little did she know, of course, that while she was playing, she was also learning about forming, testing, and adjusting hypotheses, how decisions shape and change the story, and how to take someone else's perspective, all valuable historical thinking skills.

History has remained an ongoing interest. I wrote a couple of novels and several books for children on subjects ranging from T.E. Lawrence to the Boer War, and I briefly taught Grade Twelve history at a downtown Toronto school, but it was only when my daughter started kindergarten that I looked more closely at what schools here in Ontario would be teaching her for the next twelve years (since education is provincially mandated, I refer mainly to the Ontario curriculum, but the truth is that Canada's other provinces follow a very similar syllabus). I was struck by the yawning absence of history in the early grades ("History" as a subject is only introduced in Grade Seven), and its extremely narrow focus and disconnectedness in middle and high school. This bothered me as a narratologist, but it also bothered me deeply on a personal level and I began to wonder why it shouldn't bother other people, too.

So, this is a book intended for the general reader and for anyone with an interest in how we talk about the past and how we use it to build our future. If you are a parent, student, teacher, activist, consumer, or voter, this book is for you. Many of the issues I explore will be all too familiar to history teachers and curriculum specialists, but my hope is to move these discussions into the public sphere. I don't presume to write as an historian, educational specialist, or policy maker, but rather as someone with a love for story and a deep belief in the power and value of historical literacy. Neither I nor any of the experts I've spoken with would argue for a return to how history used to be taught; we would, however, advocate for a return to how it used to be *valued*.

Curriculum design is a politically charged subject in most countries, and Canada is no exception. If there is one common assumption that I would most like to knock into the long grass, it would be this: that anyone who endorses teaching more history to our children must by definition be conservative and Christian, not to mention likely male and a subscriber to one of the nuttier homeschooling programs. I am none of these things. Over the course of my voting life, I've cast ballots for all four major parties. I am also an atheist, a woman, and a public-school parent. These details may seem irrelevant, but anyone who has spent more than a few minutes following any education scrum on Twitter will know that they are not. I share them here to indicate that my passion for promoting the elevation of diverse, wide-ranging, global history in our schools is not motivated by political or religious ideology, but by a love for the subject and an ardent belief that our children and our society can only be enriched by learning more of it.

As this book entered its final edit in early 2022, evidence for the continuing relevance of history continued to mount. In 1996, Thomas Friedman noted that two countries which both had a McDonalds wouldn't go to war: their societies, the assumption went, would be too wealthy and have too much to lose. That prediction has since been disproved, perhaps most shockingly with Putin's recent invasion of Ukraine. Suddenly, history was in the news again, as observers started brushing up their European history to draw comparisons with the Second World War and projecting the likelihood of this conflict turning into World War Three. Twitter buzzed with pundits observing that "history repeats itself" had taken on surprising new resonance: "I wasn't expecting all of the twentieth century in two years," remarked one.

Some of the research for this book was originally completed for an article I wrote in 2018, although the project has expanded since then beyond my focus on history teaching in Ontario elementary schools to include movements and perspectives from the U.S., Australia, and the U.K. As a result, the book in your hands features the voices of world-famous historians, award-winning teachers, and leading educational innovators, as well as everyday parents and students; men and women, young and not so young, from a range of ethnic and cultural backgrounds. I've striven to incorporate a wide range of opinions and perspectives, which, of course, means there is plenty of room for disagreement and debate. Nevertheless, one thing that all my interview subjects share in common is the belief that now, more than ever, we need *more* history, and we need to centre it more prominently in our school curricula and broader conversations. What follows, then, is a call for the elevation of history above the improvised, politicized hodgepodge that we currently call "social studies," and for its restoration, through a coherent, intentional approach from the earliest grades right up to postsecondary level, to the centre of education. It will be no mean feat, but it can be done.

Here's how.

I

WHAT'S AT STAKE

Why History?

“IMAGINING THE FUNCTIONALITY OF a human being without historical sense is really scary.”

It was an uncharacteristically grim observation made by my old college tutor, Dr. Perry Gauci, during a Zoom conversation in the summer of 2020. My peers and I had always regarded Perry as indefatigably cheery: his infectious grin had reassured and encouraged me through my first round of Oxford interviews, and his pre-exam pep talks were as energizing and inspiring as the best cornerman encouragements. But what he'd said also made complete sense at a moment when the world felt as if it were teetering on the brink; when many of us were at once scrambling to try to see into the future while maintaining some semblance of normality in the "now." Imagining a human being without historical sense *is* scary. The thought of living exclusively in a blinkered present moment is scary. Scarier still is the thought of an entire generation, not to mention society, operating from a position of historical ignorance. And yet that is exactly the situation in which we find ourselves today.

The people and events of history may be rooted in the past, but how we talk about those things, what we write about them, and how we teach them (in other words, how we *practise* history as the record of human experience) tell us a lot about who we are and what we value right now. It's easy to think of all those who came before us as either foolish or luckless enough to have lived in a time that's not the present. But conditioning ourselves to believe that we're the exception is, at best, a naïve and, at worst, a fatal mistake. Thinking of ourselves as a chapter in an as-yet unwritten history book, on the other hand, is likely to force deeper self-reflection: Whose stories will we champion? What values will we defend? What models will we offer ensuing generations? In an era of environmental change, rising inequality and seismic shifts in the international political arena, we need to understand how our institutions have developed in order to understand why they don't always have adequate responses to these crises.

History gives us this power. No other subject helps us to understand so comprehensively what it is to be human. No subject is more vital to our very humanity.

That's why it was so shocking to read, in September 2020, that almost two-thirds of surveyed Americans between the ages of eighteen and thirty-nine did not know that six million Jews were killed during the Holocaust, and more than one in ten believed Jews caused the Holocaust.[4] In a survey commissioned by the Conference on Jewish Material Claims Against Germany, the *Guardian* reported, 23 per cent of respondents said they believed the Holocaust was a myth, or had been exaggerated, or they weren't sure. Twelve per cent said they had definitely not heard, or didn't think they had heard, about the Holocaust.

The implications of this kind of ignorance are staggering, but the ignorance itself isn't entirely surprising given the downgraded status of history in most schools. Here in Canada, the Ontario social studies curriculum for Grades One to Eight contains not a single mention of the Holocaust.

In early 2022, the cost of this became frighteningly clear. In January, several participants in the so-called Freedom Convoy to Ottawa displayed flags and signage bearing swastikas. The following month, the Friends of Simon Wiesenthal Centre called on the Toronto District School Board (TDSB) to recognize anti-Semitism as a "crisis" after another alleged incident at a middle school. The organization's president and CEO, Michael Levitt, said in a release: "Anti-Semitism has reached epidemic proportions at TDSB, and it is time for the board to recognize this as the crisis that it is. It is unfathomable and shocking that, in 2022, a Jewish teacher is faced with Nazi salutes and a 'Heil Hitler' chant in her classroom. Clearly, something is broken in Toronto's public school system and requires immediate attention."[5]

(And yet debates about the "age appropriateness" of teaching the Holocaust persist. The same month, a Tennessee school board banned a Pulitzer Prize-winning graphic novel about the subject, *Maus*, on the grounds that it included "inappropriate language," nudity [there is one instance of a nude woman, depicted as a mouse], and discomfort around depictions of violence. Board members expressed concerns that eighth graders would not be able to handle such material.)

It's dispiriting, to say the least, to realize that we are sleepwalking towards becoming a Visigoth state like the one described by Neil Postman. "[For] the Visigoths," he wrote in his popular and widely circulated graduation speech, "history is merely what is in yesterday's newspaper."[6]

If you're reading this, chances are you already know that history is much more than that. It is, in fact, everything and all of us: it's quite literally inescapable. As educator and author Susan Wise Bauer observes in *The Well-Trained Mind*, history isn't just a subject: it's *the* subject. "Unless you plan to live entirely in the present moment, the study of history is inevitable,"[7] she writes. For many, myself included, history is inherently, inevitably, and infinitely compelling, but there will still always be those who question its "usefulness."

One simple answer is that historical knowledge is power: the control of history, which shapes our political and cultural identity, is precisely why cathedrals of knowledge from the Library of Alexandria to the Library of Congress (and from Catholic collections during the Reformation, to Jewish collections during the Holocaust, to Islamic collections during the Balkan wars of the 1990s) have been targeted for destruction and appropriation since earliest times. "There is no political power without power over the archive," observed Jacques Derrida[8]: ancient Mesopotamian rulers used the texts preserved in their libraries to decide when to go to war,[9] while today authoritarian regimes and major technology companies vie for control of the archive as it migrates to a digital realm.

On an individual level, studying history gives us roots: a context for our existence. Individuals who lack that context lack a significant element of self-understanding but also an understanding of their relationship with the rest of society. Rootlessness limits our ability to function, to empathize, to feel invested in anything beyond our own immediate needs. It also disempowers us. Powerless people become easy targets for exploitation, propagandizing, and manipulation, particularly by those who appear to offer membership to a group or cause. As Professor Bob Bain (whom we'll be hearing from more later on) put it to me, "Stories help orient us to the present. If you've got no story, then you're primed for someone else to give one to you."

Not surprisingly, there's a great deal of skittishness over the idea of teaching children any kind of agreed-upon narrative, because no one wants to be accused of forcing the "wrong" kind of story on impressionable minds. But the result of teaching no coherent story at all is a fragmentation of knowledge, what Bain described to me as "the by-product of a generation of people like me who were taught that any grand narrative is manipulative, paternalistic, and evil, without realizing how necessary it is."

There's an obvious tension at play: on the one hand, we need history to build understanding and appreciation for shared values and responsibilities, while on the other we need to remain vigilant against distortions that create an oversimplified narrative; the kind that, as renowned historian Margaret Macmillan writes, "flattens out the complexity of human experience and leaves no room for different interpretations of the past."[10] In her brilliantly concise and accessible *The Uses and Abuses of History*, Macmillan details many examples of such a flattened history: from the nineteenth-century Grimm brothers collecting German folk tales to prove that there was such a thing as a German nation dating back to the Middle Ages, to dictators including Robespierre and Pol Pot creating new calendars to begin history afresh, and Mao and Stalin writing their enemies out of the record. The BJP government has consistently attempted to rewrite history to present India as a Hindu nation from its earliest beginnings, while here in Canada, French-Canadian nationalists have often focused on the past as a story of humiliation at the hands of the British while neglecting examples of cooperation (for instance, over the building of the railways and through the early years of Confederation) or, indeed, French-Canadian sympathy for a rival foreign government during the Vichy regime.

More recently, the trend in the West has veered the other way, towards deconstructing and challenging inherited national narratives in pursuit of a type of historical catharsis. So, do we teach history to build a sense of national pride, or to poke holes in it? As Daniel Immerwahr wrote in the *Washington Post* towards the end of one of the most tumultuous years in living memory:

I teach history, and such questions have always struck me as odd, for two reasons. First, we design curriculums around what students will learn rather than how they'll feel. The aim of a geometry class is not for students to love or hate triangles but to learn the Pythagorean theorem. Similarly, the point of U.S. history isn't to have students revere or reject the country but to help them understand it.

The second reason is that, by imagining history class as a pep rally or a gripe session, we squeeze the history out of it. The United States becomes a fixed entity with static principles, inviting approval or scorn. And that makes it hard to see how the country has changed with time.[11]

Clearly, in an age of "fake news," Google, and Wikipedia, engaged citizens need to be culturally literate, critical thinkers. There is no better subject than history to develop an appreciation of context and an ability to interrogate evidence. Just as we expect a math curriculum that systematically builds on blocks of knowledge and developing skill sets, we should also expect a logical history curriculum (preferably an international one) for our children. If it were commonplace to hear graduates claim that they'd never learnt to divide, there would be an outcry. So should there be now.

Such knowledge-based learning needn't tell students *what* to think, but would rather provide the tools to learn *how* to think. In the digital age, perhaps more than ever, "users" (to adopt the purposefully dehumanizing tech term) require a sense of sequence and consequence, a nose for collecting sound evidence, and an ability to discern the difference between sophisticated and oversimplified analogies. To look something up, you need to know what you are looking for. And in these hyper-partisan times, history reminds us of the importance of nuance and the enduring fact that there will always be contradictions. No single group is right all the time, and we all need to be able to hold two opposing ideas in our head at once.

Furthermore, as Professor Faith Wallis, a medievalist based at McGill University, posited in conversation with CBC Radio's Nahlah Ayed, it's worth asking "What makes true history in an age of fake news, when fake news can elide into fake history . . . and where fake history can be amplified so widely?"[12] Wallis went on to describe two accidental discoveries she'd made online, shortly before the discussion: one of a deep-faked Victorian photograph that had been digitally animated so that it appeared to come to life, the other of a deep-faked news broadcast by Richard Nixon announcing the failure of the Apollo moon landing and the deaths of the three astronauts on board (the text was taken from a speech that had been drafted in case the mission failed, but was never used). The implications of digital technology to rewrite history convincingly and of social media to amplify incorrect history to a wide audience are obviously deeply concerning. "Ignorance is bad, [but] false certainty is perhaps even worse," Wallis warned.

For this reason, the role of historical experts has never been so important in the battle against facts that have been distorted, ignored, or passed through heavily biased filters. Harvard's Professor Jill Lepore echoed Wallis' concerns by observing that most political claims in America today are currently made with reference to history, but without a true appreciation of historical process and nuance: "There's a general degradation of the idea that there is historical truth to be found," she said. And today's popular appetite for history as entertainment doesn't always translate into an engagement with deeper questions or appreciation for the historical process.

It's easy to reach the exhaustion point: to throw up our hands in despair at the relativism of everything. Lynn Hunt captures this problem beautifully in *Why History Matters*: "If it is so easy to lie about history, if people disagree so much about what monuments or history textbooks should convey, and if commissions are needed to dig up the truth about the past, then how can any kind of certainty about history be established?"[13] The fact remains that, imperfect though it is, we need historical truth. Without it, Hunt points out, we have no leg to stand on to counter the claims of dictators or Holocaust deniers.

But just what exactly *is* historical truth? The concept is as slippery and evasive as ever, although most would agree that it boils down to actions or events, and arguments as to their causes and consequences, which can be verified by historical *evidence*. As the evidence changes, so must the story. Of course, our knowledge of what happened in the past will always be incomplete and contestable; partly because it's impossible to access every thought or deed of every person who has ever lived, but also because our understanding of the past relies not only on facts (which do not change and which can be objectively verified) but also on shifting *interpretations* of those facts, both by contemporaries of any given historical moment and by their successors. Historical truth cannot, therefore, simply be reduced to "the facts": establishing the facts is an important first step, but equally important is the distillation of *meaning* from these facts.

This, of course, is not always a straightforward exercise. Often, the available evidence (for instance, a letter), as well as interpretations of this evidence (an historian's reading of that letter) is inherently value-shaped: it reflects feelings and beliefs which may shed important light on a subject without themselves being universally or objectively true. Values shape our understanding of historical truth, but they are not the same thing as historical truth. Values shift, whereas truth does not. Historians' work will never be done, therefore, because the stories we record and interpret are in constant need of correction, adjustment, and reinterpretation based on the available evidence. And the questions they ask will necessarily keep changing, because we're always wanting to ask questions that are relevant to the present. As Julia Lovell, winner of the 2019 Cundill Prize for her book, *Maoism: A Global History*, explained in a panel discussion with fellow shortlistees, "Historians always have to answer the 'So what?' question."[14] Traditionally, the questions posed about nineteenth-century China could often be reduced to "Why did it fail so badly?", but now, in light of China's rise to twenty-first-century superpower, that question has become "How can we find the seeds of China's contemporary success in the nineteenth century?" Evidently, the practice of history teaches us a number of things: not least, flexibility, patience, humility, and the value of keeping an open mind.

In 2014, leading historians David Armitage and Jo Guldi (from Brown and Harvard Universities) wrote in *The History Manifesto*:

> What sort of an education prepares individuals for so volatile a run through the journey of life? How does a young person come to learn not only to listen and to communicate, but also to judge institutions, to see which technologies hold promise and which are doomed to fail, to think fluidly about state and market and the connections between both? And how can they do so with an eye to where we have come from, as well as where we are going to?[15]

In their book, Armitage and Guldi identified a telling shift away from over-specialization in the academy back to longer-term narratives (the *longue durée*, as it's also known). Later on, I'll be talking about the appeal of such "big picture" history for students from kindergarten through university. The long and short of it is that students who don't have this sort of "big thinking" awareness are unlikely to be able to escape "the conceptual fetters of the present moment" (to quote historian Sanford Jacoby). Digestible narratives that sensitively incorporate up-to-date research are urgently needed to help us make sense of the environmental, political, economic, and moral challenges facing us today.

* * *

The good news is that the public appetite for history has never been greater. Anthony Wilson-Smith is president and CEO of Historica Canada, an organization devoted to promoting an understanding and discussion of Canadian history. The fabled Heritage Minutes, commercial-length history lessons blending re-enactment and narration, are arguably Historica's greatest achievement, reaching about 27 million users annually. The first ones aired in 1991 and featured Valour Road, the Winnipeg location that was home to three Victoria Cross recipients; the Underground Railroad, which brought runaway slaves to freedom; and Jacques Plante's invention of the goalie mask. Lines such as "Doctor, I smell burnt toast!" and "I'll need those baskets back," quickly entered the cultural lexicon of many young Canadians. One of my friends, of South Asian heritage, said that the Minutes (in particular, the one about the Chinese workers who build the railroads) did more to teach her about diversity in Canada than anything she learnt in school in the 1980s and 1990s.

In May 2020, Wilson-Smith told me, a new Minute about Canada's role in the liberation of the Netherlands seventy-five years ago "shattered all our previous online viewing records, despite the near-absence of the heavy media coverage we usually get when we release." The minute was seen more than 4.2 million times online in the first thirty days of release; the previous record (for a D-Day Minute in 2019) was 3.4 million.

Current events have also informed a spike in interest. "We track the top five most-read pieces every week in the Encyclopedia," explained Wilson-Smith (Historica Canada operates Canada's national encyclopedia on a digital platform that can be viewed at thecanadianencyclopedia.ca). "At the outset [of the Covid-19 pandemic], pieces on the 2003 SARS outbreak and the 1919 Spanish Flu routinely made the list. Once the public focus on BLM and Indigenous rights and discrimination erupted, we saw an immediate spike in related stories. For more than ten weeks, articles on residential schools and Black history in Canada (including pre-Confederation slavery) have been among the top five."

The success of the Heritage Minutes illustrates the potent combination of human interest and contemporary relevance in making history appealing. Curiosity about the past often starts on a personal level, which perhaps explains the explosion of interest in ancestry websites, DNA test kits, and TV shows exploring celebrities' family histories. The sensational success of the musical *Hamilton* illustrated the power of a compelling and important story, creatively told (the main character might be a dead white guy—a lawyer, banker, and politician, to boot—but a largely rap-based score and majority Black cast brought fresh appeal and insights to a new generation of audiences).

More conventional productions have also proved to have a wide reach: Ken Burns' documentaries have long attracted impressive viewership numbers, as did Mark Starowicz's *Canada: A People's History* when it was released in 2001. Reviewing the latter in the *National Post*, Robert Fulford may have criticized the series's portentous tone ("as if all those people lived through four centuries or so without once cracking a joke") and clichéd narration ("rebellion is brewing, the die is cast, cholera spreads like wildfire . . . It's like having captions for Matisse written by Tom Clancy . . .") but conceded that "even raising such questions about the approach and the writing style . . . acknowledges how important it is."[16]

"Reality" series featuring historical re-enactments–families "sent back in time" to experience life as pioneers or on the home front during the Second World War–as well as computer games, Netflix series such as *The Crown*, and historical fiction also indicate the enduring claim of history on the public imagination. This appeal starts young: several years ago, our daughter discovered my childhood collection of American Girl books, which followed the adventures of (admittedly extremely monochromatic) pioneer child Kirsten, Edwardian beauty Samantha, and 1940s schoolgirl Molly; she later encountered a new generation of characters, including Nez Perce Kaya and freed slave Addy. Contemporary children's literature continues to add a rich tradition of historical fiction: to old favourites *The Silver Sword* and *The Egypt Game* can now be added *Percy Jackson & the Olympians* and *I Survived*. Criticisms are sometimes directed at the place of historical fiction in the classroom, but writers such as Afua Cooper tend to dispel the notion that academic historians can't also produce meaningful historical fiction for young people. The founder of the Black Canadian Studies Association and a leading scholar on African Canadian studies, Dr. Cooper's young adult novels, *My Name is Henry Bibb* and *My Name is Phillis Wheatley*, tell the stories of children from the Black diaspora. (The same holds true for adult historical fiction: David Diop's remarkable *At Night All Blood Is Black* recounts the experience of a Senegalese soldier fighting in the trenches during the Great War; it won the International Booker Prize in 2021.)

Tales such as these provide inclusive representation as well as a picture of the grand patterns of human experience. "People are trapped in history and history is trapped in them," wrote African American novelist James Baldwin in his essay "Stranger in the Village." There's a comfort in the sense of order that can be imposed on the past, particularly when our own times seem to be characterized by great upheaval and unpredictability.

* * *

So what's the bad news?

In short: plummeting history enrolment at universities, concerns among practitioners that the subject is fragmenting beyond recognition, and students who don't recognize themselves in the history they study at school and can't connect the disconnected fragments they *have* learnt. In the coming chapters, I'll be looking at what has caused this disengagement, why it matters, and why some trends in historical teaching might be doing more harm than good.

There's been plenty of hand-wringing in Ontario over nosediving elementary math scores, with only half of Grade Six students meeting the provincial standard in 2018. By comparison, there's been resounding silence around another subject in which elementary students have long fallen behind. By now, you can probably guess which subject that would be.

But it's STEM jobs that are hiring, we're told. "Historians make lattes," was the wry observation of one history teacher I spoke with.

Certainly, schools are getting much better at teaching previously overlooked aspects of our history, including Indigenous history (which the last curriculum overhaul made compulsory) and social history. But these bits have been superimposed on a disjointed, incomplete curriculum—a curriculum that, as it stands, doesn't only threaten to kill off student enthusiasm for history as a subject but sends them into the world with huge knowledge gaps (more on this in Chapter Two).

It's a muddled curriculum, pieced together by the separate agendas of politically capricious governments, boards, and education departments. It's a timid curriculum, reluctant to embrace the conflict, collisions, controversies, and paradoxes in history. It's a curriculum heavy on centering "deep dives with lots of primary sources," as Professor Bain described equivalent America syllabi to me, but one shy of providing a connected overview, leaving these projects "like postholes with no fences to connect them."

The alternative doesn't have to be a return to "rote" learning, but rather a joined-up attempt at building broad knowledge from the earliest years to create context for understanding later on. When history is only introduced as a subject in Grade Seven, after which it's limited to a couple of years of Canadian history taught largely outside of any kind of chronological or global context, the results aren't surprising: students enter middle school without any sense of the "story" of history, high school teachers despair that students come to them without the knowledge or skills to learn how to think historically, universities experience plummeting numbers of history applications, and, in turn, we as a society become increasingly ahistorical in our outlook, not to mention distressingly polarized in our discussions of such things as the toppling of statues (again, more on that later).

The problem is not limited to Ontario schools. At the time of writing, New Brunswick was embarking on a high school history curriculum overhaul with an eye to diversifying and expanding its offerings (a full K-12 curriculum revamp hasn't been attempted in that province in almost half a century). Improvements can't come soon enough for Karen Robert, chair of the history department at St. Thomas University. "They come to a place like St. Thomas, where we emphasize a more global history curriculum, and we end up having to start from scratch to just introduce them to even basic world geography," she said in a CBC report.[17] "There are ways that political systems can break down, can slide into dictatorship, can slide into mass human rights violations . . . Is it inevitable? No. But if you don't have any historical perspective, you don't even see the warning signs."

Gary Waite, history chair at the University of New Brunswick, echoed Robert's concerns about a lack of knowledge among students. "We have to do a lot of remedial work overall," he said.

Readers of a certain age may remember the lively debate that arose in the 1980s around a writer and academic by the name of E.D. Hirsch. His breakout book, *The First Dictionary of Cultural Literacy*, occupied a privileged place on the shelf at home when I was growing up. Far from being a narrative or a chronology to be dully memorized, it offered up a tantalizing, eminently "dippable" collection of people, places, mythologies, and historically significant events that, taken together, would provide the kind of knowledge that even as a child I sensed could unlock layers of meaning in the world around me. They were also par excellence an example of diversity, showing how cultures have interacted over many millennia, sharing and contesting ideas, stories, and guiding beliefs.

Hirsch's central argument, over the course of several bestselling titles, has been that the knowledge gap is as much an enemy to equity in our schools as the computer gap. Knowledge-rich learning, according to Hirsch, is in fact the best hope we have for a more informed and equal society, because it equips all students with shared reference points that can help us to speak a common language. Although he acknowledges the importance of student-centred learning to build engagement with a subject, Hirsch also emphasizes the importance of encountering broader narratives, which can open us up to a greater range of experiences.

(In *Reaching Mithymna*, his account of time spent among the volunteers and refugees on the island of Lesvos, writer Steven Heighton reaches a similar conclusion about Greek culture. A chance conversation with a stranger in a café about a possible relationship between the name Theseus and the Greek word for sacrifice, *thysia*, leads Heighton to observe that "Greece teems with 'common people' who know their own language and culture better than most academic specialists in North America know theirs. Which may in fact be the precondition for a living culture: that its knowledge be democratically distributed, not confined to an elite who address mainly each other in a kind of gated dialect."[18])

"In the nation as a whole there is now a knowledge gap, a communications gap, and an allegiance gap. We don't understand one another; we don't trust one another; we don't like one another."[19] This is Hirsch writing about America in 2020, though much of what he describes could equally be applied elsewhere. A loss of cohesion, Hirsch argues, is the partial result of "a loss of commonality in what we teach and therefore in what we know." If change is to happen, it needs to happen with coherence, commonality, and specificity. "When one school adds certain lessons for the sake of diversifying its curriculum and other schools add different lessons of their own, we're left with divided citizens who cannot communicate with one another, because they don't have enough knowledge in common."

We pay a certain lip service to this idea by framing history as a part of "civics" education, but the fact is that it is so much more than this. The title of this book refers to a "vanishing" past not because history itself is going anywhere, but rather because the discipline of history has become so segmented, sidelined, and co-opted for other purposes. "History fights for its place in the curriculum with civics and geography," Professor Bain observed during our conversation, "but its attention to time, place, and context is what makes it really distinct."

Others agree. Writing about history teaching in Quebec, Marc-Andre Ethier and David Lefrançois have argued that "History teaching itself should not be subjected to citizenship aims. Rather, civic competence should arise from historical competencies . . . [which] also make possible other ways of thinking about the world."[20]

In other words, history doesn't simply *tell* us how to be good citizens: it equips us with the knowledge we need to comprehend our world clearly, and the ability to analyze it accurately.

"Precision is not a skill: it's a value, an obligation, a moral duty," observed Dr. Gauci towards the end of our Zoom conversation. The skills versus knowledge debate is an old one in history teaching, and generally it's a misleading one: you need both to do history properly. Dr. Gauci worries about how little many students seem to know about the political process, as well as about limited public discernment when it comes to discussions around current events. But history, to him, is about even more than this.

"It's always been the instinct of many of the most creative minds to look back," he said, and here I was pleased to see the old smile return. "The great dreamers all needed the past. *We stare into space and we wonder*, so it seems strange not to do it in the rear-view mirror, too."

Whose History?

I N OCTOBER 2020, CBC reporter Omayra Issa tweeted about Tobi Omofeya, a young man from Regina who launched a petition to get more Black history taught in Saskatchewan schools. The petition received nearly 73,000 signatures, marking a significant step in the ongoing struggle for Black people to be officially recognized in the education system.

Too often, we merely pay lip service to underrepresented and marginalized histories: Black History Month, for instance, is regularly presented as disconnected from the "rest" of history and risks implying that African American history begins and ends with slavery and the Civil Rights Movement. Within Canadian history, the recent emphasis on Indigenous voices is also long overdue. But using history simply as a place to acknowledge the wrongs of the past indicates a piecemeal approach to curriculum reform; a feel-good Band-Aid in place of an emergency heart transplant.

To fully appreciate the vast arc of human interaction, engagement, conflict, cruelty, retribution, and reconciliation, we need to widen our ambitions. Absent a coordinated curriculum, time-strapped or less imaginative teachers will reach for the same stories to tick the Black history box: the Underground Railroad, Viola Desmond. The same goes for Indigenous history, which until my daughter reached Grade Three was limited to discussions about wampum belts and residential schools. The last curriculum revision in Ontario took place in 2018, shortly after the Truth and Reconciliation Commission published its Calls to Action. As a direct result, requirements for teaching Indigenous history were added, but in practice much of the history that has been stressed is one of victimhood rather than Indigenous resistance, resilience, and success (the Ontario social studies curriculum for Grades One to Eight, which makes only seven references to slavery and none to the Holocaust, mentions residential schools fifty times).

Teachers such as Christina Ganev seek to change that. A TDSB Hybrid Teacher-Coach who has also contributed to the NFB, Elections Canada, and the CBC *Secret Life of Canada* teaching guides, Ms. Ganev was one of the 2020 finalists for the Governor General's History Awards for Excellence in Teaching. Anti-oppressive and anti-racist teaching is at the heart of what she does, and she sees a vital role for history as a subject in making schools more tolerant places.

"Global history education can be used to build inclusion, foster empathy, strengthen democracy, do reconciliation work, and inspire good local citizenship. For me personally, [it's] critical to anti-oppression and anti-racist pedagogy," she wrote to me in an email. "A robust knowledge base of history that is not Eurocentric can ground students and help them to understand current issues and the state of the world today. Schools reproduce colonialism and white supremacy, but that is being examined, and it is changing."

The challenge, according to Ganev, is that "textbooks and teacher training programs have not yet caught up with these changes. Since many teachers were students in schools where [marginalized] histories were not taught, the onus is now on them to unlearn, relearn, and teach in a different way as school boards have failed to provide such professional development." Providing teachers with resource support to help them teach sensitive material is one of Ganev's projects: by preparing pre-approved teaching packages that might include sample letters to parents, a calendar of topics, and language terms, she hopes to help advance teacher confidence in tackling important topics.

Of course, it's not only teachers who have a significant amount of relearning to do. As Dorothy Williams noted in her landmark book, *Blacks in Montreal 1628-1986*, "There is a prevailing belief among the general populace that Blacks are Canada's newest immigrants. This assumption remains despite the burden of proof to the contrary."[21]

Natasha Henry, an educator, historian, and curriculum consultant specializing in the development of learning materials that focus on the African diasporic experience (she's also the president of the Ontario Black History Society) is currently building a database of enslaved people in Ontario. Teachers cleave to the curriculum as the "official" history, she says, and any other stories tend to be brought in at their discretion as add-ons. As a result, students lack opportunities to contextualize their experiences as part of a broader story.

In conversation with curriculum specialist Samantha Cutrara,[22] Henry noted that there are no learning expectations about Black Canadians that all Ontario students must cover (there is indeed no standardized curriculum for teaching African Canadian history in any of Canada's provincial systems), something which she believes "leads to institutionalized erasure." For this reason, she wants to see Black Canadian history mandated in the curriculum (at the time of writing, Markiel Simpson is leading a similar call in British Columbia). During the Covid-19 pandemic, Henry said, more African Canadian families have been "deliberately choosing to use Afrocentric approaches at home to teach their children," being more intentional in discussing Black experiences in response to a failure of schools to offer the same. What still isn't clear is whether the "return to normal" after the pandemic has ended will also mean a return to white-dominant narratives.

It's true that Canada provided the last stop in the Underground Railroad, a network that helped enslaved people escape to freedom. But teaching only this narrative carries two risks: first, of perpetuating white-saviour messaging, and second, of overlooking Canada's own part in the slave trade, which only ended in 1833 when slavery was abolished across the British

Empire. Until then, advertisements for buying and selling slaves made regular appearances in early Canadian broadsheets, and Canada participated in a wider network of international trade connections that made slavery possible. No fewer than nineteen slave ships were built in Newfoundland, and salt cod was regularly sent from Atlantic Canada to the West Indies to feed enslaved people working on the sugar plantations that provided refined sugar for Canada's rum distilleries.

"The arc of this country is that we generally get better on human rights issues over time," Historica's Anthony Wilson-Smith told me. "We can take comfort from that, but not too much, because history also shows us we're never as good as we think we are."

Never was this as true as in May 2021, when the remains of two hundred and fifteen children were located on the grounds of a former residential school in Kamloops. The discovery, which was followed by similar findings at other sites in the months that followed, was devastating but not surprising to those familiar with the histories of residential schools, including Indigenous community knowledge keepers. In response, the Canadian Historical Association (which represents 650 professional historians) published an open letter on Canada Day maintaining that the historical record proved that genocidal intent lay behind Canada's past treatment of Indigenous peoples.[23]

Soon after, a counter-letter was released, signed by roughly sixty academics from institutions across the country. Their position? That reducing history to a single message sacrifices healthy debate while ignoring complexity and detail, the very things that drive historical investigation. "The Council of the CHA claims that 'the existing historical scholarship' makes it 'abundantly clear' that Canada's treatment of Indigenous peoples was genocidal and that there was 'broad scholarly consensus' as to the evidence of 'genocidal intent,'" it begins.

> The CHA Council also attacks the profession in stating that historians have turned a blind eye to the tragedies that have marked Canadian history. There are no grounds for such a claim that purports to represent the views of all of Canada's professional historians.

While the signatories to the second letter insisted on a commitment to ongoing interrogation of the history and legacy of residential schools and encouraged all Canadians to read the TRC's final report, it took issue with the assumption of a unanimous academic view on the subject. Monolithic, morally superior readings of the past aren't what history is about, they imply. The intentions may have been good, but the presentation of a "consensus" view of history was not. The letter continues,

> The CHA exists to represent professional historians and, as such, has a duty to represent the ethics and values of historical scholarship. In making an announcement in support of a particular interpretation of history, and in insisting that there is only one valid interpretation, the CHA's current leadership

has fundamentally broken the norms and expectations of professional scholarship.[24]

As we approach the question of how to teach the darker parts of our shared history, it's worth acknowledging the fact that historians themselves are often at odds with the best way to go about this!

It's good to see many discussions around the teaching of Indigenous history beginning to take centre stage. In his article "Teaching History from an Indigenous Perspective: Four Winding Paths up the Mountain," the late UBC Indigenous scholar Michael Marker explained that the problem isn't simply a lack of Indigenous content, but "the deeper problem is that the categories of what counts as history do not often correspond with the ways that traditional indigenous [sic] communities make meaning out of the past." In other words, Indigenous time and knowledge systems are frequently overlooked or misunderstood, meaning that conversations around Indigenous history are always passed through the distortions of a Eurocentric lens. Marker continued:

Cherokee author Thomas King has written that "the truth about stories is that that's all we are." There is a deep and dangerous purpose in narrating the past, and Indigenous people understood this well. A wrongly told story–and by this I do not mean strictly inaccurate–could have devastating consequences for a village, since people made important survival decisions based on their reading of the environment and on the oral traditions that referenced sacred relationship with the ecologies of the past.[25]

What does this mean for teachers? For one thing, it might require recognition of Vine Deloria's critiques of the Bering Land Bridge theories, which many Indigenous groups reject (oral histories maintain that they've been on the land since the beginning of time); it might also mean addressing the cognitive geography of Indigenous peoples whose ancestral land is now divided across the provinces and between the U.S. and Canada. And it could include recognizing the four paths described by Marker as central to Indigenous ways of knowing: the centrality of circular/cyclical time, relationships with land and animals, holistic local knowledge, and the complexities of colonization and decolonization.

That may sound like a lot to process, but it's necessary, and it's overdue. Professor Robert Bothwell is a noted expert on Canadian political and diplomatic history. As he observed during our conversation, "In most histories, the Indigenous peoples disappear after 1815, and that's wrong." At the same time, he warns, it's vital that we stress stories of triumph as well as mistreatment. Approaching Toronto from the north, along the Don Valley, it's hard to miss the Foresters Company building. "That company was founded by a Mohawk (Dr. Oronhyatekha)," he told me. It's a valuable example that "there were Indigenous people who were very successful in larger society, and it's unfortunate that we ignore this."

There's a clear public taste for these stories, which schools can and should be capitalizing on. Earlier in 2020, actor Dan Levy shared an Instagram post inviting his fans to join him in studying Canadian Indigenous history. Roughly 64,000 people signed up for the online course offered by the University of Alberta, which offers both historical content and lessons in Indigenous ways of knowing and learning. Faculty reported never having seen anything like that kind of enrolment, which came just as the U of A announced that it would be merging faculties in response to devastating provincial funding cuts.[26]

Changes are afoot at all levels of schooling. In Manitoba, Métis and First Nations communities gathered in November 2021 to celebrate the building of a tipi at each of the elementary schools that offer its pre-kindergarten program. The principal of École Saint-Lazare, Richard Fiola, explained in an interview that "our school board, DSFM, offers a pre-kindergarten class in schools that do not have a daycare. We are integrating young children as early as four years old to learn French and participate in our culture. During Covid, we have chosen to release quite a few projects outside. The tipi is to add a new area to do outdoor teaching."[27]

He went on: "We hope to be proud of our origins, as we are a little Métis community here but we want to also recognize the First Nations that are our neighbours. We want good relations, we want to acknowledge that we recognize errors of the history but we want to write the pages for the next century on a good basis."

Meanwhile, in northern Quebec, a new history curriculum has begun making its way into some Cree high school classrooms. The new curriculum, developed by the board, teaches history from a Cree perspective (the board received a derogation from the Quebec Ministry of Education for this to happen). "We're looking at history from an Eeyou perspective and as a way to support identity construction of our students," said chairperson Sarah Pash. "We know that our students have very different needs from students in the south . . . It's really time now that our children hear our own stories from our own mouths, from our own perspectives."[28]

The life and work of Louie Kamookak stands as another example of how Indigenous oral history not only helped solve a major Canadian mystery but engaged wider public interest in Indigenous knowledge. Most famous for his part in the 2014 discovery of *HMS Erebus*, one of polar explorer Sir John Franklin's lost ships, Kamookak was also involved in a project to collect Inuit knowledge around the doomed expedition, knowledge that had been passed down orally through generations. Two years later, *HMS Terror* was also located using testimony from Inuit elders. Both ships had been part of Franklin's 1845 search for the Northwest Passage. Kamookak was recognized with the Order of Canada; in an interview, he said that the project played an important role in recognizing "our amazing ancestors that once lived where no other people chose to live."[29]

Kamookak, who died in 2018, was not an academic historian, but increasing numbers of Indigenous scholars, following in the path of renowned Metis historian Olive Dickason, are forging a place for Indigenous history in the academy as well as the mainstream. Bestsellers such as *An Indigenous People's History of the United States for Young People* (based on Roxanne Dunbar-Ortiz's bestseller, adapted by Jean Mendoza and Debbie Reese) reframe language in a way that forces readers to recast what they think they know about Indigenous history. Mendoza and Reese make a point of not italicizing non-English words in order to avoid "othering" those languages; the index lists individuals with information about their nation, citizenship, or country (George Washington, therefore, is described as "Euro-American, U.S.," while David Archambault is described as "Standing Rock Sioux Tribe"). The authors also provide excellent background on European explorers, tracing the impetus for Western expansion right back to the Middle Ages. This isn't revisionist history or history that aims to elevate one group over another: this is complete history.

There is always a risk of presentism–the reading of history through the lens of current events–which good history (and good history teaching) must seek to avoid. As Lynn Hunt writes in *History: Why It Matters*, "The dose of presentism cannot be too high or it will lead us to commit anachronism, that is, the failure to respect chronology. Then the past just becomes an inert mirror of ourselves . . . But the dose of presentism also cannot be too low[:] would we want to judge Hitler as just another politician?"[30] In the move to address the whitewashing of history as it used to be taught, history today is sometimes discussed as an extension of civics; but reading history backwards produces little of value in terms of students' ability to understand properly and come to terms with the past.

Nowadays, "presentism" can become a politicized and highly contestable term to throw into discussions of how we talk about history; as one curriculum expert I interviewed quipped, "Presentism is used as a cudgel to bang down ideas [Conservatives] don't like." The same interviewee observed that "someone who pulls down a statue is reinterpreting history, albeit in a violent way." It's an interesting argument, although it perhaps excuses some elision of the grey zone that exists between historical interpretations. In June 2020, for instance, nearly a hundred and fifty years after the abolitionist Frederick Douglass spoke at the unveiling of the Emancipation Memorial in Washington, D.C., a group of Black Lives Matter protesters attempted to topple the memorial's statue, which depicts Lincoln and a freed slave. Many considered Lincoln's service to African Americans to have been over-inflated; others objected to the portrayal of a free black man kneeling before the president. In the end, the memorial stayed in place (although a facsimile in Boston was removed from public view several months later). Many now argue that the statue, which had originally been paid for by freed slaves, is a valuable part of Black history itself and should remain as a testament to their experience.

With this in mind, perhaps a worthier target than presentism would be *a priori* reasoning. As Professor Bothwell wrote to me: "You have to teach your students respect for evidence and hence, truth (of course, this puts one at odds with those who follow

Foucault—and there are many, many of these in academe)." Good history doesn't allow us to assume foreknowledge. It reminds us that history isn't inevitable, no matter how familiar some stories may seem (indeed, the stories we take for granted, such as the rise of the Nazis, are perhaps the ones that most demand constant refreshing). Bad history, on the other hand, tells incomplete stories: "It makes sweeping generalizations for which there is not adequate evidence and ignores awkward facts which do not fit. It demands too much of its protagonists, as when it expects them to have had insights or made decisions that they could not possibly have done. The lessons such history teaches are too simple or simply wrong," as Margaret Macmillan writes.[31]

Interpretations of how history should be presented may not always fall neatly along political lines. Bothwell pointed out that "the Tories lavished $20,000,000 on [Canada Hall at the Canadian Museum of History] and got a panorama of political correctness" that's "pedagogically ineffective, because there's nothing to talk about." But certain historical flashpoints will always guarantee to evoke strong feelings. Outcry over systemic anti-Indigenous racism led to the toppling of statues of Canada's first prime minister, John A. MacDonald, as well as the removal of his name from the law school at Queen's University, sparking heated public debate. On the one side were arguments against erasing the past (and questions as to the manner in which the statues were removed; in Montreal, the damage in question was done by members of a "de-fund the police" protest, inviting unanimous condemnation from the leaders of the Liberal and

Conservative parties and premiers across three provinces); on the other, counterarguments that history doesn't reside in statues but in stories and understanding (interestingly, a 1997 Dominion Institute survey of eighteen to twenty-four-year-olds found that only 54 per cent knew who John A. Macdonald was, begging the question: Has the next generation been better instructed in school, or were the statue-topplers acting on knowledge acquired through other channels?).

(Meanwhile, Library and Archives Canada quietly deleted a website titled *First Among Equals*, which listed biographical information about each of the country's prime ministers. "[The site] is outdated historical content that no longer reflects current understanding of history," a spokesman said. But instead of updating the site, it was scrubbed completely, and users are now instead directed to a page of primary documents to do their own research.[32])

The legacy of Confederate statues erected during the Jim Crow era (not to mention the statues of slave-owners demolished in Bristol and Antwerp) differ significantly from Victorian homages to Canada's founding PM, and the anti-statue movement has been a largely visceral and spontaneous one, which makes explaining it a challenge and therefore ripe for oversimplification.

When is beheading a statue a righteous act, and when does it become an act of wanton vandalism (as when the Taliban blew up statues of the Buddha in Afghanistan in 2001)? Should Macdonald's Indigenous policies outweigh his broader legacy? Does it matter that he wasn't the father of the *Indian Act* (that actually happened on Liberal PM Alexander Mackenzie's watch), given that he still supported the residential school system? Is it possible to respect political institutions while reviling the founders of those institutions?

Few of the heroes we venerate for bringing about positive change in their time were without any moral stain. Abolitionist William Wilberforce opposed working-class suffrage. Gandhi, while practising as a lawyer in South Africa, disparaged black Africans and argued in favour of racial segregation. Mother Teresa opposed measures that would have fully emancipated the women in her care. Their good works in other areas do not exonerate them for these failings, and the same may well be said to apply in reverse (this is not an argument in favour of moral relativism: an individual whose driving ambition was to suppress, subjugate, or destroy a particular group of people obviously shouldn't be considered in the same category of personalities). We need to be able to hold two ideas in our head at the same time. Indeed, this may be our best defence against the dangerously simplistic and reductionist thinking of our polarized age.

Stanford education professor Sam Wineburg quotes two excellent examples from American history to help challenge monolithic interpretations of great men (and women). One is George Washington's address on Oct. 3, 1789, in which the first American president announced the modern holiday of Thanksgiving. The speech includes multiple references to a "great and glorious Being" and "Lord and Ruler of Nations," and at first glance reads to modern eyes as drippingly pious.

Without any background knowledge of the vast melting pot of religious denominations in post-Revolutionary America, students could well mistake this for the speech of a country preacher, and not a highly attuned leader using eighteenth-century linguistic codes to keep his references to God intentionally vague in order to appeal to Catholics, Jews, Protestants, and freethinkers. In this case, Wineburg writes, "close reading . . . can't compensate for ignorance."[33] You've got to understand the context of the speech before you can draw conclusions about its speaker.

Similarly, a speech in which Abraham Lincoln appears to defend racial inequality can easily prompt students to lurch in horror: Was the Great Emancipator, in fact, a white supremacist? Look closer, though, and we'll see that the speech was delivered during a senatorial debate, in a location known for anti-Black sentiment, in front of an audience largely supportive of his opponent; in short, he was courting votes. The words may taint our picture of Honest Abe, but they also can't necessarily be taken at face value as representative of his own personal beliefs.

Nor can we allow our explanations to be oversimplified. Wineburg recalls a classroom discussion in which a question about an historical instance of racial injustice was answered with one word: it happened, a student suggested, because of "prejudice." "Four hundred years of racial history reduced to a one-word response?" Wineburg ponders. How to teach students that we need to think historically about things like prejudice, racism, tolerance, fairness, and equity? "At what point do we come to see these abstractions not as transcendent truths soaring above time and place, but as patterns of thought that take root in particular historical moments?"[34]

Historians know the importance of historical distance; of recognizing the ways that specific events are influenced by wider discourses. Learning to think historically means learning how to identify the biases that inform how we tell certain stories. Sometimes they are obvious, as when U.S. President Donald Trump, in his 2020 Fourth of July speech at Mount Rushmore, announced the creation of a statuary park honouring "American heroes," a group of mostly white men. A month later saw the launch of the 1619 Project, an endeavour intended to reframe American history by changing America's founding date from 1776 to 1619, the year that twenty African slaves were brought to Jamestown, Virginia. Although the latter project has been enthusiastically welcomed, it has also ignited debate as some academics have challenged the reframing of the American Revolution as a slaveholders' rebellion, the alleged minimization of connections between Black activism and other radical movements, and the project's implicit denial of the importance of change over time (by suggesting that racial inequality is programmed into the DNA of American history, impossible to recalibrate). Still other academics admitted to harbouring factual objections to the project, while disagreeing with attempts to challenge it as an unnecessary escalation of an already highly charged discussion.

Other critics have noted that the 1619 Project risks treating slavery as a uniquely American phenomenon while also ignoring the Native American origin story. And there are those who disagree with elements of presentism in its approach. In an interview with the *Paris Review*, Black attorney, historian, and author Annette Gordon-Reed observed that 1619 is not necessarily more important than 1776. "As a teacher, I want students to think about contingencies," she said. "I didn't think it was right to bring the American founding dilemma back to a moment in history at which people would not have recognized that dilemma. The people who were here in 1619 were Englishmen, and Africans had been enslaved for centuries by the Portuguese, the Dutch, the Spanish, the French. The quandary for the republic arose when someone said, 'All men are created equal,' and the person who wrote this owned slaves. But in 1619 there was no inkling. The United States was not inevitable in 1619. Nothing was foretold."[35]

One solution might be to consider a more global, long lens approach to teaching the histories of minority groups and those that have suffered systemic oppression. Instead of starting Black history with the trans-atlantic slave trade, we might consider teaching children about great African achievements that predated it—the Iron Age ruins of Great Zimbabwe, for instance, where artifacts have proved the existence of a complex trading network extending as far as China; or the Mali Empire of Mansa Musa, widely regarded as the wealthiest ruler of the Middle Ages. Teaching the horrors of colonialism is necessary and important, but so is promoting an appreciation of the sophisticated civilizations that existed before European nations took over. Rather than beginning narratives with empire and exploitation, which is still a way of telling these stories through a white, European lens, we could instead first introduce stories of cultural vitality and celebration. These can and should be followed by stories of resistance and creation, such as that of Toussaint L'Overture and the Haitian Revolution.

(I stress Black history here because it is a particularly timely subject at the moment of writing; but, of course, the same should be said of a wide number of cultures and traditions whose members make up the rich fabric of our society today. For instance, Islamic history could and should be centred in the same way, beyond Islamic History Month, to celebrate the rich scientific, artistic, and cultural contributions of Islamic civilizations.)

Implicit in all of this is the idea that Westerners don't have a monopoly on historiography. There is an ancient tradition of written history in China, for instance. Historical narratives take a range of forms across cultures, too: from the knotted *quipus* of Incan tradition to Indonesian sung narratives, and in those cultures that view history cyclically, where history is imbued with prophetic qualities.

History isn't a project in civics or political rehabilitation, and it can't be reduced to mere tokenism. Perhaps this is why there was something slightly confused about the #BlackedOutHistory campaign, in which pictures were taken of an Ontario history textbook with all the parts not relating to Black Canadians struck through. This left only thirteen pages of the textbook material legible; a number that does fall grossly short if the struck-out bits only related to white, Anglo history. But many of these sections would presumably have included Aboriginal and other diaspora and immigrant histories, too. We risk embarking on a slightly slippery slope by demonstrating that studying other groups is antithetical or mutually exclusive to knowing the histories of our own. Representation matters, and it must be improved, but the answer is not to shrink history. Dismissing certain histories as "too white," as some critics have charged classical history, conveniently forgetting the vast diversity that was one of the Roman Empire's strengths, risks cutting off our nose to spite our face (this is not to deny the very real problem of white supremacist groups appropriating classical, Viking, Anglo-Saxon, and even medieval histories to suit their causes). The better answer, surely, must be to include *more* history.

Subaltern histories, social histories, Black histories, Great Man histories, political histories, Marxist histories, Indigenous histories, women's histories, LGBTQ2+ histories, Asian histories, Muslim histories, micro- and macro histories–none should be off-limits. By teaching students to embrace the paradoxes of history and the great historiographical controversies of past and present, we can equip them to evaluate different accounts of the same events. Just as playing with 3D glasses and coloured plastic sheets reveals a new image every time the colour changes, so can we learn how changing our interpretative lens reveals new perspectives.

The problem is, we can't fit this all into a Grade Ten Canadian history class, which is currently the only high school history course that's mandatory in Ontario. We've first got to recognize that history matters enough to be a central subject in school starting in Grade One. We should be starting with stories—*all* the stories—in order to give students the time to digest and absorb valuable knowledge in order to finally be able to interpret those stories in a critical and empathetic way. Instead of continually adding Band-Aids to stick the historical Humpty Dumpty back together with a veneer of diversity and reconciliation, we should instead be bold: we should be rethinking how we present the entire subject from the ground up.

An excellent example of how *more* history, mindfully and coherently presented, can help to resolve deep divisions can be found in Israel, where Sami Adwan at Bethlehem University and Israeli psychologist Dan Bar-On collaborated on a project culminating in a bi-national, Israeli-Palestinian history textbook. Recognizing the challenge of reaching a consensus on a common interpretation of the Middle East conflict, and supported by the Georg Eckert Institute for International Textbook Research in Brunswick, Germany, a team of teachers and scholars produced a text in which both narratives are taken separately into account, illustrating the conditional nature of diverging interpretations (so, for instance, what is described as a "national catastrophe" by one side is depicted as a "War of Independence" on the other side). The book came out in America in 2012 as *Side By Side: A Parallel History of Israel-Palestine*, and stands as a powerful example of an expansive, creative, and constructive approach to presenting a troubled historical relationship that endures to this day.

We've got to engage our heads and our hearts when it comes to addressing historic injustices. Being an ally is easy when you not only understand context but have a developed sense of empathy. Cultivating imagination is a big part of this (just think of Maya Angelou's tongue-in-cheek suggestion that Shakespeare was, in fact, a Black woman!). Stories grow wonder, and wonder sparks imagination. Being able to place ourselves in someone else's shoes is what makes us empathetic humans: this is why we should, for instance, insist on teaching boys about the extreme trials of the suffrage movement, as well as the fact that it wasn't just a part of "women's history." They themselves could once have been prohibited from voting on the grounds of class, race, and income, too.

Rethinking and decolonizing school curricula is a necessary first step. But many critics who are keen to see a standardized curriculum to address the problem of minority group erasure are, at the same time, deeply opposed to mandating knowledge (or "content") more generally. As the next chapters will show, this is largely for political and ideological reasons, not convincing pedagogical ones. Until we recognize the need for a bold expansion of historical knowledge across the board as the necessary foundation of the development of critical thinking skills, we're unlikely to be able to move toward a more understanding, integrated, and just society.

II

WHAT'S MISSING

When was History
demoted, and why?

I N RECENT YEARS, university enrolment in history
majors has slid farther and faster than any other humanities
discipline. A report from the *Economist* indicated that the
number of students studying history in the U.K. declined by
10 per cent over the last decade. In the U.S., the figure is a
staggering 30 per cent. Anecdotally, the trend is likely similar
across Canada, although lecturers at York and Waterloo say
their numbers are even worse.[36] While this decline became
most marked after the 2008 financial crisis amid employment
concerns and the saturation of teaching jobs, it also speaks of a
much wider disengagement with the subject.

(The problem isn't exclusive to the western hemisphere:
in June 2020, Australia's federal government announced that
the cost of studying humanities at university was set to double,

but that "job-relevant" course fees would be slashed under an overhaul of tertiary education. Courses in agriculture, maths, science, health, environmental science and architecture [among others] would be cheaper, while fees for humanities courses would see more than a 100 per cent increase. "Students will have a choice," the education minister said. "Their degree will be cheaper if they choose to study in areas where there is expected growth in job opportunities."[37])

The real problem isn't to be found at the undergraduate level, however, but rather in our elementary and high schools, where history is woefully neglected. Instead of despairing about tuned-out eighteen-year-olds, we should be firing up the interest of eight-year-olds. In 2018, I conducted a small-scale survey of Grade Six and Seven students attending a range of public, private, and religious Toronto schools, hoping to find out what they'd been taught about history beyond Canada's borders.[38] The results were eye-opening. Grade Six students couldn't say when the Second World War happened or what country Nelson Mandela came from, and Grade Sevens couldn't place Anne Frank, Marie Curie, and Martin Luther King in chronological order.

Some readers will question the relevance or usefulness of such knowledge. Technology has facts covered; teaching facts is old-fashioned. We'll explore more deeply in the next section why it's an error to dismiss "mere facts," the very bones of the stories we tell, on these grounds. First, we need to take a closer look at the status of school history today.

As recently as 2016, Ontario was lauded by Historica Canada in its Canadian History Report Card for its "rich"[39] Grade Ten compulsory credit course (admittedly, a significant improvement on 2009, when Historica's report failed five provinces and territories, and assigned marginal passing grades to two more). Look beyond the celebratory headlines, however, and you'll find that "rich" (the *Toronto Star's* term) is a byword for overstuffed: in the one year that Ontario high school students are required to learn history, they must cover both world wars, twentieth-century immigration, the Cold War, the Korean War, the FLQ Crisis, the Charter of Rights and Freedoms, the OPEC crisis, and the Meech Lake Accord, to name just a few topics (let alone Black, Indigenous, and other histories that are now rightfully expected to be incorporated). As Anthony Wilson-Smith noted at the time, a course of that scope would be much more effectively spread over two years (many history teachers agreed). Perhaps more pressingly, think of all the history that it still *doesn't* cover: everything pre-1914, not to mention most of the world beyond Canada's borders.

One obvious problem is that history as a subject is only introduced in Grade Seven. Before then, the Ontario elementary curriculum (and most provincial curricula across the country—Ontario, Alberta, and British Columbia follow very similar programs) offers "social studies," which is almost exclusively Canadian in focus. The only compulsory, non-Canadian material appears in Grade Four (as part of "Early Societies, 3000 BCE-1500 CE") and Grade Nine. According to the official curriculum document:

"The social studies program in Grades One to Six develops students' understanding of who they are, where they come from, where they belong, and how they contribute to the society in which they live. Students develop a sense of who they are by exploring their identity within the context of various local, national, and global communities in which they participate."[40]

Citizenship has long been a major part of the social studies curriculum (although, interestingly, no student I interviewed in 2018 was able to identify ancient Greece as the birthplace of democracy). Sound historical knowledge is fundamental to building an appreciation of diversity and an understanding of power relations. But historical scholarship and good citizenship are different things; using one simply to serve the other hearkens to a time when history was taught primarily as part of the nation-building project. Admittedly, that identity crisis is perhaps the reason that the current curriculum is almost exclusively Canadian in focus. In Grade One, children learn about "The Local Community"; in Grade Two, it's "Changing Family and Community Traditions." Grade Three introduces "Communities in Canada" as well as "Living and Working in Ontario." In Grade Four, students are at last introduced to "Early Societies, 3000 BCE–1500 CE." But then in Grade Five, they return to Canada with "New France and Early Canada." And Grade Six wraps up with "Communities in Canada" (does this sound familiar?) and "Canada's Interactions with the Global Community."

But wait, there's more. Grades Seven, Eight, and Ten also focus exclusively on Canadian history, leaving just Grade Nine, and optional courses in Grades Eleven and Twelve, for the rest of the world to get a look in. (I approached the Ministry of Education on several occasions to request to speak to anyone involved in curriculum design to comment on, among other things, the logic of spending four years on a narrow window of Canadian history before reverting to the Middle Ages, but never received a reply that addressed these questions. The one reply I did receive essentially confirmed that the curriculum is as I've described it.[41])

I'd like to pause here for a moment to note that plenty has already been written about the teaching of history in Canadian classrooms, but that most of this writing has been (and continues to be) by educators, for educators, and limited to a fairly niche world of blogs, academic conferences, and university press publications. I carry no particular expertise or desire to wade into these debates, but I do think it's important that general readers hear more about them. And there are few comprehensive overviews as succinct or convincing (not to mention refreshingly free of orthodoxy) as Bob Davis' 1995 book, *Whatever Happened to High School History?*

Despite the crusty title, Bob Davis was no throwback. One of Canada's leading educational thinkers and teacher activists, Davis was a long-time Toronto high school history teacher who also taught at York University. He wrote frankly about his broadly socialist leanings and was perhaps best known for spearheading the teaching of labour history and his introduction of two Black history courses in the 1980s and 1990s (he taught at Stephen Leacock C.I., which at the time had a roughly 15 per cent African Canadian student population).

Davis is excellent at explaining how history, once considered "queen" of the social sciences, underwent decades of erosion from the 1970s on: initially as part of a drive to propel a stronger sense of Canadian national "identity," and later through a trend toward a more sociological emphasis and learning that emphasized skills over content. But far from simply bemoaning the subject's decline from core subject in the 1960s to a mere minor option in the 1990s (where it remains today), Davis held out hope that it might be revived as a core subject at some point in the future. That moment could be now.

Ironic as it may seem, history is a relatively new subject. In the Middle Ages, theology was king. Later, classics and the Bible formed the cornerstone of any elite Western education. It was only in the nineteenth century that history became codified for instruction: first, for the sons of the rich (who mainly studied the histories of Israel, Greece, Rome, and the British Empire as tales of imperial pride and progress), but later as a beacon for a wide array of groups that included Marxists, people of colour, and liberal and progressive thinkers. As tax-supported schooling extended across Europe and North America, this story of history-as-progress became a popular way of growing loyalty to government and free enterprise. Davis writes: "The whole story was to be held together as an account of the progress of a certain class, sex, race, and nationality–in the case of Upper Canada and later Ontario, white English bourgeois males."[42]

This was not a species of history for which Davis advocated: indeed, he was up front about the fact that "the canon of 1960 was elitist, imperialist, pro-capitalist, patriarchal, racist, Anglo-biased, patronizing of Quebec, and pro-American." Over that decade, various "curriculum-focusers" including the early Canadian anti-nuclear movement, Quebec nationalism and Canadian nationalism, women's and labour movements, developing world and Indigenous voices, and youthful perspectives meant that "we could finally add units of study about these buried people and talk about the transformation of history that adding their story implied."

Sounds good, doesn't it? But this excitement was short-lived. Davis continues: "By the late 1970s and early 1980s a strange truth hit me. While we were confidently debating what the new history should look like, the subject itself was disappearing under our feet."

Why? A new focus on "core curriculum" meant increased time devoted to language and math instruction, while history became steadily consumed by sociology courses such as People in Society, World Politics, and World Religions. The new courses were fun, but they didn't leave much room for dealing with the origin of things. Previously, "the school system was still saying that at least ideally most students should be exposed to this entire evolving story, at least as far as Grade Twelve. The package was like a set of Russian dolls: you'd open them from the larger to the smaller in some grades and put them back together in others, but everyone was meant to handle the complete set."[43] From the 1970s onward, this was no longer the case.

By the 1980s, the teaching of history skills (such as detecting bias, writing essays, and conducting research) had replaced much of the substance of history, and was all covered in one compulsory course. By the time Francis Fukuyama published his controversial *The End of History* in 1989, students and teachers were primed for the educational implications: "If history itself was over, why teach it to school children?"

In Ontario, history went from accounting for 11.4 per cent of all classes in 1964 to a mere 6.6 per cent in 1982. By the 1990s, "learning how to learn" had all but replaced learning content. Davis locates part of the reason for this as a desire to avoid politically extreme positions and a general softening of emphasis so as not to offend. The results included the production of "mountains of dull books which were so cautious that they often literally made no sense (like an ancient Mediterranean without Christianity or Judaism)." One textbook, titled *The Foundations of the West*, had all references to Christianity and Judaism removed.[44]

(Disdain for ancient civilizations carries over to other subjects, too. Latin was once taught with the aim of learning about the classical world, but "when it remained merely for snobbish reasons [and to employ Latin teachers], it was newly justified as training in logical thinking."[45] The parallels with the subject of history are not hard to see.)

Davis's account of the decline of school history aligns with Professor Bothwell's experience. The rise of social history in the 1970s increasingly squeezed out political and economic history, but social history was inclined toward fragmentation and sectarianism. The general message, Bothwell remembers, became "society is oppressive."

In this climate, the publication of Bothwell, English, and Drummond's *Canada Since 1945* was something of an anomaly (the first sentence was "Canadian history is a success story," a line which reads as almost laughably positive today). Nevertheless, it sold upwards of 40,000 copies and launched the careers and international reputations of its authors. The difference then, Bothwell told me, is that audiences in those days were still huge: "There was broad engagement with history, helped by bigger book review sections, which people actually read, and an academic style that hadn't become so jargon-laden." This would all change quickly, as history at the university level was, as in the high schools, increasingly rolled into the humanities. "We haven't agreed on what to teach since the 1980s," he told me, a complaint echoed by many other academics I spoke with.

What about student knowledge coming into the universities? Student talent is as good as it ever was, Bothwell says, but language skills have declined and there are increasingly notable gaps in knowledge. In one of his recent courses at the University of Toronto, only two out of seventy third-year students had learnt some British history, and they happened to be British. Although he doesn't advocate for a return to the days of learning the hagiography of Johnny Beaver, he does believe that, without at least some wider international history, "you'll have difficulty understanding the Commonwealth, NATO, immigration after the Second World War, and even Quebec separatism."

Students today appear inclined to agree. In response to the statement "I feel confident in my knowledge of world/ international history," one Orangeville high school graduate I surveyed wrote, "Only because of my parents, who were both teachers [who] grew up in another part of the world . . . [and] my grandmother was an anti-colonialist and a promoter of independence movements."

Ken Osborne, faculty of education professor emeritus at the University of Manitoba, has written extensively on the heavily contested ground that is school history in Canada. When I interviewed him in 2018, he was quick to acknowledge declining interest in the position of international history in the curriculum. "It was never all that strong in the first place," he wrote then. "For some reason, and despite all the talk of 'one world,' internationalization, etc., the wave of concern has never stretched to include the teaching of world history."

Christina Ganev, a high school history teacher and coach, agrees that the subject has been whittled down to its bare bones. At the secondary level, she explained to me, there are a very limited number of elective world history courses (these include "Genocide" and "Ancient Civilizations"). In her words, "Since these are elective courses, most schools only offer one or two sections of each. Only students who are already keen about the study of history tend to take these courses, and enrolment is very limited. These courses also attract students who are on the 'academic' track to post-secondary school."

In other words, if you're an average student who hasn't had the good fortune to be introduced to the wider possibilities of history beyond Canada's borders (or before 1914), you'd be forgiven for thinking that history simply isn't relevant to you.

This is the case for many of our students today.

* * *

History as a subject has shrunk considerably, and what remains of it is patchy in the extreme. Scarce consistency of content across the grades means we've ended up with a scattergun approach that confuses, bores, and restricts many students. Part of the problem lies with a focus on emphasizing the teaching of skills at the expense of learning actual content. (Even then, it's questionable how well skills are being taught: an April 2019 Ontario study assessing academic skills of recent high-school graduates led by York and Western professors and conducted at York, Western, Waterloo, and Toronto [which together enrolled 41 per cent of Ontario undergraduates] found that "only about 44 per cent of students felt they had the generic skills needed to do well in their academic studies . . . and 16 per cent lacked almost all the skills needed for higher learning."[46])

Advocates of knowledge-based learning are often characterized as retrograde, dogmatic, out of tune with their students, and lacking in imagination: stern schoolmarms twitching their rulers at the first sign of independent thought. Skills-heavy learning, so the thinking has gone, is the truly empowering approach. In reality, skills teaching was an approach designed at least in part to produce what Bob Davis described as "compliant and adaptable workers for today's economic market." Capitalism, Davis wrote, "moves mass education away from knowledge and towards skills whether manual or, increasingly, mental."[47] A popular argument among educators is that teaching skills helps students to avoid being sucked in by propaganda. But "humane student citizens," which is what Davis hoped his students would become, require broad knowledge with which to think, to judge, and to create. "Lots of history and literature and films and newspapers and radio tapes and photographs are needed to enable lots of reality to make its imprint," he wrote. "To find your place in the universe is profoundly different from having a bundle of techniques in your pocket."[48]

The "bundle of techniques" to which Davis refers is at least in part a reference to "historical thinking concepts," as described in a 1996 article by Peter Seixas, a former social studies teacher and director of UBC's Centre for the Study of Historical Consciousness. Seixas's article suggested a framework for history education based on six concepts: significance, epistemology and evidence, continuity and change, progress and decline, empathy and moral judgement, and agency. The historical thinking concepts have become a central part of history teaching in Canadian high schools, and they enjoy wide support among teachers. I've taught them and think they're great, particularly in terms of helping students to frame their analysis of a new piece of evidence. They provide a sense of purpose to historical study and challenge the idea of history being a set of predetermined facts. The concepts aren't a substitute for knowledge, though, and they're not always the most direct way to introduce new topics.

Bob Davis went farther, arguing that Seixas's framework "sounds more like understanding biases in order to shoot the breeze about them." Alluding to Orwell's description of good prose being like a window pane, Davis went on:

> Analyzing the window (and your own eyes) is certainly a necessary part of looking out the window at life itself. But if our main purpose is to make students little armchair experts on types of glass, type of Windex, types of window frames and types of eyeglasses to the point where they don't get around to looking through that window at life, then we are guilty of a massive irresponsibility.[49]

It's a harsh attack, and it certainly didn't prevent the widespread embrace of the historical thinking concepts across the country. But what I think was *really* riling Davis was the broader shift toward "sociological" history: an approach that rejected narrative in favour of relativism and heavily thematic learning.

I was a beneficiary of this sociological style of instruction. After the pablum of middle school courses at my private Toronto high school in the late nineties, a Grade Ten society course was a breath of fresh air, with topics that made us feel clever and grown-up (Freud! Feral children! Camille Paglia!). History as a traditional academic subject could never be the same. In "Mod West," we were encouraged to answer questions with more questions, and it was hard to give a wrong answer. We listened to Leonard Cohen and analyzed Napoleon's leadership style using the Enneagram personality test. My final project was an extended essay on T.E. Lawrence passed under a heavily pseudo-psychological filter. As for learning how to interrogate primary sources: that was something you did in AP History (Advanced Placement exams, although American, are available for students to sit anywhere). Only a few of us took the AP, and we prepared for it outside of regular school hours.

The current generation of history teachers are also the product of this sociological brand of learning. So why is it that I find myself questioning the continuation of such an approach today? It was engaging, and it didn't stop me from studying history at a top university. What made me different?

For one thing, I was a nerdy kid. I filled in the gaps at school with lots and lots of reading (and movie and documentary watching) outside of school. I had attended elementary school in three different countries, which meant I'd received a pretty broad grounding in other national histories by the time I hit middle school. And I was frequently inclined to suspect that there was always *more* that the teachers could be telling us (I was also, almost certainly, something of a pain in the arse).

I didn't know it at the time, but the twelve aims of history and contemporary studies that guided the Ontario curriculum in those days led with this goal: that students should "develop confidence in themselves and in their ability to deal with problems in academic and everyday life and to make sound personal, educational, and career choices." As J. L. Granatstein noted in his book *Who Killed Canadian History?,* it's somewhat surprising that "to acquire knowledge of historical and contemporary societies"[50] only made it to number nine on the list of aims. But it also chimes with my experience and I suspect would still hold true today.

Granatstein's book is hampered by a curmudgeonly tone and sensitivity to what he perceives in it as an over-emphasis on "grievance history," but he makes several points that are difficult to dismiss. Today's single compulsory high-school history course *is* heavily slanted towards current events and sociology. Linking historical concerns to the present day is important, and sociological interpretations of the past certainly have their place. But if this is what students are limited to receiving, it's easy to see that it provides an incomplete picture. Granatstein also notes a perceived association between intellectual rigour and elitism, which is often in evidence in ongoing debates around streaming and curriculum design. "Content remains second to process–a distant second," he writes. "Because it is, by definition, full of content, history is no priority, especially when it is compared with trendier subjects."[51]

The conflation of content and elitism is a significant obstacle to reviving history as a subject in Canada. Twenty years ago,

Granatstein sensed that "the idea that there should be national standards in history is a political non-starter,"[52] but given the current climate of calling for decolonized and diversified history teaching to be mandated by provinces from coast to coast, there may well be the necessary energy and commitment to pursue such a project. Whether provincial ministries, city boards, faculties of education, and subject specialists can find a way to collaborate constructively to establish common standards is another question. But it's worth a try.

Other countries, including Australia, Britain, and the U.S., have considered the teaching of history important enough to warrant national discussion, and there's no reason why we shouldn't, too.

* * *

I'd like to stress again the vital fact that history teachers at all levels are passionate and knowledgeable about their subject; enthusiasm and commitment to learning is one thing that is at no risk of decline. The problem would instead appear to be that the aims of history teaching across elementary and high schools don't always connect or build upon each other as well as they might. Over the last forty years, we've seen history at school level become fragmented at the expense of continuity, and we've seen history in the universities break up into progressively more specialized niches because departments struggle to agree on what to prescribe in survey courses. Elementary teachers are limited to teaching history as a sub-topic within social studies, which means high school teachers who wish to focus on rigorous source-interrogation are frequently met with students armed with inadequate historical skills and knowledge. University lecturers, in turn, worry about students not being able to synthesize and adequately connect the big picture or relate historical topics meaningfully to the present day; as a few noted to me, students come well prepared to argue, dissect, and specialize, but not to analyze thoroughly and explain.

"There are many common gaps in knowledge," Christina Ganev told me. "[Students] are inquisitive and fascinated by history, but it seems to be taught in such a superficial manner in [the early] grades that students are wholly unprepared for the rigor of research and skill-based approach in senior history courses." And, she said, it's not just the students who struggle:

Unlike high school teachers, most elementary teachers are not specifically qualified to teach history. Some may have a history "teachable" qualification, but most do not. Teachers may not be equipped to teach the skills or even the content in the same way secondary teachers do. I find that students are exposed to a range of content and skills, but that it is not standardized in any way. It is difficult to understand whether students have just forgotten content or skills, or whether they were never taught them in the first place. In recent years, there have been (largely inconsistent) efforts to bridge the gap between intermediate history (Grades Seven and Eight) and high school history through cross-panel discussions and working groups. We need to do more of this!

The sad fact is that elementary social studies programs leave very little time for history. As Amy von Heyking argues in "Historical Thinking in Elementary Education: A Review of Research," elementary students have to cover Canadian geography and current events as well, and a jumbled approach to teaching source analysis overlooks the limited content knowledge that children are able to bring to their reading. Von Heyking notes, for instance, that "History education researchers Bruce VanSledright and Christine Kelly . . . found that students without sufficient content background or contextual information assessed the validity of a primary source by the *amount* of information it provided"[53] [my emphasis]. In order to be able to evaluate new information, it's necessary to have some previous knowledge against which unfamiliar evidence can be measured; otherwise, we're sending young children on a scavenger hunt for facts the value of which they have no ability to judge for themselves. We also need to teach a stronger grasp of time concepts and dating systems; things that aren't intuitive and need to be taught in order for children "to begin to understand the sweep of time and scale of events." Only then can they be "prepared for the idea of change as a process, not just a series of events."[54]

The arrangement of time, place, and causation are elements particular to the study of history, and yet somehow we have reached a stage where chronology isn't part of most curricula.

Indeed, any form of larger national narrative is anathema to many elementary curriculum specialists today. I questioned one curriculum expert about this on Twitter; he went so far as to say that elementary students "don't have a conceptual foundation" for any kind of political or diplomatic history, "in addition to its being culturally biased."[55] (I'm still not entirely sure what this last point means, or how cultural bias ceases to be an issue when studying history later on, but I was reluctant to split hairs at the time.)

I had wanted to know if it was true that Grade Two students couldn't be expected to learn about ancient China and Rome, as he had mentioned in a CBC interview commenting on leaked Alberta curriculum proposal documents (more on those later). "Trying not to be obtuse," I wrote, "but just looked at the doc. The bits about Chinese history mention dynasties, building the Great Wall, silk and spices trade, Marco Polo, Chinese explorers. Are seven- and eight-year-olds not ready for these topics?"

"Correct," he replied.

I asked him what aspects of Chinese history he believed they would be ready for.

"Daily life," was the answer.[56]

The thing is, as any historian will tell you, "daily life" is hard to discuss without at least some framing. I also struggle with the idea that emperors, wars, trade (of goods, yes, but also of enslaved peoples), and explorers are beyond the grasp of most eight-year-olds. A friend's third grader could tell you plenty about double agents, Pearl Harbour, the Nepalese army and the bombing of Burma. But, thanks to the dominance of certain curricular orthodoxies, any child keen to study history in any sort of depth has to do so outside of school hours.

To me, this sounds like squandering the peak "sponge" years, not to mention depriving our kids of the thrill of asking big questions and empowering them with the knowledge and techniques to start answering them. How can we expect anyone, of any age, to make sense of the present without some grounding in the past?

Instead, the current focus in most North American public elementary schools is on what curriculum designers call "horizon building." In our household, we call it "four years of All About Me school projects." The thinking is that you start by getting kids comfortable talking about themselves and their families before broadening out to discussions of their neighbourhood and local community. Kindergarteners (or older kids, particularly those in French Immersion–my daughter was in Grade One) learn about "community helpers" such as firefighters and police officers (but, as one critic pointed out, how many kindergarteners aren't already familiar with the concept of a fire station?). Horizon building has come in for increased criticism in recent years, however, as more experts call for an approach of "scale switching" instead (this would jibe with Lynn

Hunt's call for "histories that are deep and wide and histories that are minutely particular and histories of dimensions and units in between because we live in a world of many dimensions, from the local and the national to the global"). In the current system, between JK and Grade Three, my daughter completed five timelines about her life to date, all virtually identical, but for the addition each year of one new significant event.

In those earliest years, with the exception of books shared in the library or the occasional visiting speaker, there was no real opportunity to touch on mythology, biography, or bigger moments in world history; no stories of heroism or adventure or exploration, of overcoming adversity or creating works of great beauty, of bringing positive change to the world or of growing through mistakes. We did, however, spend one freezing afternoon in Grade One traipsing around the neighbourhood taking photos of my daughter in front of the fruit market and the bank to establish that she did, indeed, know that these things were part of her community.

We have been blessed with excellent teachers: warm, wise, knowledgeable, creative, and passionate about learning. They have challenged and supported and enriched our daughter's education in many ways. Not for one second do I blame the myopic focus and repetitiveness of "horizon building" learning on them. Nevertheless, the fact remains that it is a "virtually content-free"[57] approach, to borrow the words of educational historian Diane Ravitch. And, as a 2003 report from the Thomas B. Fordham Institute concluded, this kind of early years learning about the world lays precisely zero groundwork for the later study of history–not to mention the fact that "children tend to find its narrow focus deeply boring."[58]

More pressingly, writes author, historian, and educator Susan Wise Bauer, "History learned this way makes *our* needs and wants the center of the human endeavour. This attitude is destructive at any time, but it is especially destructive in the present global civilization." Instead, "from a practical point of view, starting the curriculum with ancient history makes sense," because there is so much to capture the imagination of six-year-olds: "The average first grader would much rather read about the embalming process than go on a field trip to his local center of government."[59]

There are shoots of hope. Quebec's elementary curriculum directly cites as its aim "the development of historical thinking and the acquisition of the method of establishing historical knowledge" as well as "seeing events in terms of continuity [and] the ability to put things in perspective . . . to situate events in a temporal context."[60] It provides as one example the study of Iroquoian society in its territory around 1500 and comparing this with territorial changes by 1745. Comparisons are also made to certain aspects of Inca society around 1500, as well as between colonial Canadian society and the Thirteen Colonies. This kind of specific attention to place, context, and sequence, not to mention a broader outlook that explicitly invites comparisons with other civilizations, is not at all typical of other provincial curricula. Quebec's high school history and citizenship course is also impressively wide-ranging, building cumulatively from Athens and Rome, through the French and American Revolutions, to colonization and civil rights. Such a course should, arguably, be required at high schools across the country. (It's interesting to note that, in a recent survey, a majority of Canadians voted the Indian Act as the most important event in Canadian history; Quebec was something of an outlier, with a majority of Quebecers continuing to place the Battle of the Plains of Abraham in top position).

Where we go from here will be the subject of the final chapter, but first it is worth inspecting how current discussions about the teaching of history are playing out in schools (as well as in curriculum-planning departments and provincial ministries, not to mention online), and to what effect. There's far less agreement than one might expect, as well as a heck of a lot of political rhetoric.

Armour up: this is the bit that gets contentious (and sometimes personal).

What's working, and what isn't?

IN OCTOBER 2020, a Twitter thread by a history professor at Western University caught my eye. It was remarkable for its even-handed summary of the current discourse around how we value and teach history. Graham Broad wrote:

> I agree wholeheartedly with those who say that we need to teach more Indigenous history and Black history and women's history. AND with those who say we need more top-down history of Prime Ministers.
>
> Everybody thinks their particular discipline doesn't get taught enough, and polls of general knowledge in any field always produce depressing results. Most people don't know about basic science, geography, history, civics, etc.

But historians have a special case to make here because we barely teach history *at all* in Canada. Students get a couple of classes K-12 and of the third who go to university, maybe 10 per cent take a history class.

Given that so many of our current societal priorities are framed historically—that is, they concern how we understand the past—there's an urgent requirement to change that.[61]

The thread also caught the eye of a curriculum expert at UBC who disagreed with Broad's point that we barely teach enough history. Lindsay Gibson's defence of the status quo seemed to clash with the view of every other history teacher I'd spoken to. I asked Gibson if I could follow up with him to better understand his perspective, and he kindly agreed.

The importance of history is woven into learning throughout the grades, he told me, even if it isn't given an explicit place in the curriculum; this is particularly true in British Columbia, where he's based. As for *how* it's taught, that's something for curriculum experts to determine: historians are experts in their subject, but not necessarily in how to convey it to school-age students, Gibson argued. This is part of the reason why historical thinking concepts have become central to history teaching across Canada: "because they're profoundly pedagogical." And, yes, Gibson admitted, they were originally seen as "a way of sidestepping the political debates of what content to teach," although we've now reached a point "where we do have to have discussions about content."

I pressed him on that problem of politicization: to an outsider's eye, ideologues would appear to make themselves as comfortable in faculties of education and curriculum design as they do in government ministries of education. In such a climate, how can we ever hope to escape politicization of debate? First, Gibson says, we have to ask if we want an *informational* or an *educational* approach to history at school level; the latter being less about building up knowledge and rather about developing "a more nuanced understanding of how history works." It's all part of learning that, for instance, "a statue isn't history; it's an interpretation of history." Considering his laudable resistance to binaries (be it the done-to-death skills v. knowledge debate, or the slightly less well-worn themes v. chronology discussion), Gibson's reference to an informational/educational dichotomy seemed stark: yet another either/or proposition in a field that remains surprisingly attached to with-us-or-against-us thinking. It's difficult to argue with the suggestion that education should be about learning to think, and not just filling up young minds with bits of information. What it doesn't acknowledge, however, is the need for an informational base with which to think meaningfully and deeply.

(It's also worth noting a distinction between the history one has to know to be an informed citizen and educated person, and the skill of building and interpreting history as professional historians do. Law school largely involves studying cases, learning the Charter, and building a foundation of knowledge about legal materials [although yes, these materials change]; young lawyers actually learn to *practice* law only when they begin articling. For all the talk about teaching kids to "think like historians," we might be reminded that the study of history works in a similar fashion.)

The disagreement between Broad and Gibson captured for me one of the great divides in current discussions about history: namely, between historians and curriculum experts. In many cases, provincial curricula are shaped largely by educational specialists, with subject specialists (such as historians) chipping in. This is perhaps not surprising, and not in itself a bad thing. But problems arise when curriculum designers, whose driving focus is on *how* students learn, take charge of discussions that allow limited input from those with a range of views on *what* students need to learn to succeed in life beyond school. This could be the main reason we haven't been able to move beyond the skills/knowledge debate, although most people on both sides frequently and correctly observe that the debate itself is a red herring.

Classroom teachers often end up caught in the middle: increasingly encouraged to promote broader, more diverse, and inclusive histories, and to emphasize development in critical thinking skills, but poorly supported in terms of training and resources, and tasked with students who increasingly arrive at high school with patchy historical knowledge. (The gap between education researchers and teachers themselves is significant, according to Daniel T. Willingam and David B. Daniel: "In theory, the goals of education research are to build knowledge and improve decision-making and outcomes for teachers and students," they write. "But in practice, education research is shaped by the common practices and priorities of researchers, not teachers or school and system leaders."[62])

A telling discussion between teachers was featured on TVO's *The Agenda* with Steve Paikin, in two episodes that aired on March 6 and April 22, 2014. Here is part of Paikin's conversation with Ruth Ann Turnbull, a retired teacher from the Simcoe Muskoka Catholic District School Board:

> RUTH: The emphasis on literacy and numeracy has pushed everything else to the side. I don't think this year, with the coming anniversary of the First World War, especially in the elementary panel, there is a move to recognize that anniversary. The last year I taught–
>
> STEVE: Wait a second, can I stop you there? We're 100 years–we're almost 100 years from the start of World War I and nobody's learning about this in elementary school?
>
> RUTH: No, because Canadian history in the elementary panel ends in 1914.
>
> STEVE: It ends in 1914.

Contributions from high school history teachers Neil Orford (a Governor General's History Awards Recipient) and Andrew Lynes highlighted similar problems at the secondary level:

> ANDREW: One of my biggest criticisms of history in high school is that there's just not enough of it. You only have to take the Grade Ten course. And that's Canada in the

twentieth century. So that leaves out Confederation, and you do that when you're thirteen years old in Grade Eight. And I don't know . . . you're not at the age where you can really understand what's going on in Confederation at that point. I mean, I think it's really important to teach it throughout elementary school to get a primer . . . moving forward to that you can deal with it at a deeper level in high school. But a lot of people just basically haven't really dealt with that on a deep level at all.

NEIL: There is such an opportunity in elementary school to bathe and nurture the child in wonderful historical moments . . . and then it becomes such a rich experience for those kids.

What, of course, doesn't happen is we don't make the transition to high school for history students particularly easy. Years ago, when I started, there was still British history in Grade Nine, and you had it not to inculcate them with British values but because you had to teach the architecture of Canadian government and what the state was all about . . . We've really compartmentalized education now by doing a little of this, a little of that, and a little of that.

STEVE: That's not good.

NEIL: It's not good for anything. If you were training to be a mechanic, you wouldn't want that kind of opportunity to be a mechanic. We don't do it in a particularly thoughtful or meaningful way for the evolution of a child's thinking.[63]

The sample group of students that I surveyed back in 2018 would appear to agree. They consisted of kids attending generally well-resourced schools, a mix of public, private, and Catholic. A mother who answered my call for volunteers via a Facebook parents' group replied within minutes of showing her Grade Six son questions on the Second World War, the end of apartheid in South Africa, and the Middle Ages: "He said he has not been taught ANY of this [and would] just be guessing! Some may ring a bell, but not because it was taught in school . . . He says they have covered First Nations and New France and have yet to start history this year." Another mother reported that her middle schooler couldn't answer a single question because the only history that she had studied in any depth was Jacques Cartier. One middle schooler identified the Raj as "the guy who built the Taj Mahal."

One Grade Twelve student was also keen to join the discussion. "I think the main issue with the way history is taught is that the dots aren't really connected," she told me. This student was taking world history at a progressive, selective downtown Toronto public high school, and was therefore able to put the French Revolution, Russian Revolution, and Chinese Cultural Revolution in chronological order. But, she admitted, she wasn't sure about the correct chronology for Abraham, Jesus, and Muhammad (included not for theological purposes but because this sort of sequence is foundational to beginning to understand cultural politics and ongoing conflicts in the Middle East and beyond).

Across the country, many highly qualified, dedicated instructors are teaching history units in thoughtful, creative, and engaging ways. The problem does not lie with them. The problem lies in the absence of any single, overarching vision of the value of history, of its central place among subjects, and of continuity of instruction across the grades. Inconsistency, the result of politically capricious curriculum changes, and a lack of resources also need to be addressed. Many teachers I spoke with have to base their classes largely on what can be found on Teachers Pay Teachers and by internet surfing; self-translating and photocopying materials is particularly common in French programs, as so few new textbooks also exist in French. In December 2020, the *Toronto Star* reported that the auditor general had found a worrying proportion of Ontario textbooks were outdated in many subject areas, a finding that wasn't news to most teachers. "In fact, 15 per cent of curricula subjects taught in the province were developed and put into practice at least 15 years ago (2005 or prior), and an additional 51 per cent were released between ten and fourteen years ago," starting in 2006, the report found. A spokesperson for Education Minister Stephen Lecce responded that the government is focused "on ensuring the curriculum we teach our children is modern and focused on developing the skills they will need to succeed in the job market and in life" and has "placed a major emphasis on STEM education and ensuring our students are well rounded by being emotionally intelligent, financially literate, technologically savvy, and ready for the jobs of tomorrow."[64]

The same evening that I came upon Graham Broad's thread on Twitter, I spotted an unrelated post by a high school history teacher asking for opinions on beginning her Canadian history course with the Cold War instead of World War I and World War II, because the Cold War, in her view, seemed more clearly linked to "modern history" and contemporary events. She later deleted this tweet, possibly chastened by reminders that 1919 laid the groundwork for geopolitical divisions that endure to this day, and that social identities from women to Indigenous groups were forged during the Great War. But even teachers with a more confident grasp of significance and sequence struggle, partly as a result of the popular trend toward thematic teaching. Chronology and themes should work together; but if thematic teaching becomes over-emphasized, and all sense of chronology is lost, we risk ending up with what Professor Bothwell described to me as "bits and pieces history."

One of Bothwell's former PhD students, Trish McMahon, is now a research lawyer and coordinator of the oral history program for the Osgoode Society for Canadian Legal History. When I spoke with her, her sons were in Grade Seven and Grade Five. Both love history (they attend the Royal Ontario Museum's Summer Club most years). Her younger son attends a Montessori school, which McMahon says has delivered a very global curriculum with a broad sense of chronology: the Grades One to Three curriculum starts off with the general and circles back with more specific details in Grades Four to Six. By the time students reach middle school, they will have covered ancient civilizations through the twentieth century, with a focus on Canada in more recent years.

Her older son, on the other hand, attends a school that follows the Ontario curriculum and is taught history as part of a "humanities" course. He's studied New France through the War of 1812. "Aside from what we talked about at home, there was no 'global context' or even a sense of empire when those topics were covered," McMahon told me. "In Grade Eight, there's more Canadian history. In Grade Nine, it's an interdisciplinary approach that includes Canadian literature, history, and geography. Again, not much about the world or Canada's place therein."

In McMahon's view, a sense of global history is profoundly important to Canadians, "perhaps more so than for other countries, because we, as a country, are shaped by international forces; [we're] the product of the French and British empires and international conflict; we're a middle power next to a superpower, [and we've] been populated through waves of immigration." But that's not what most schools emphasize, and in her view it's to the detriment of students. The undergraduates that she taught "lacked a sense of chronology and narrative . . . This isn't to say that local history or micro-history doesn't matter but learning either without context misses the forest for the trees. History does happen chronologically, not thematically."

Rose Fine-Meyer, a lecturer in the master of teaching programme at OISE and another recipient of the Governor

General's History Awards, agreed that the narrow focus is a problem when I spoke with her in 2018. "I tell my students, 'Grade Four is when you've got to travel the world: it's your only time to leave Canada!'" Starting with a local lens has its benefits, of course, but "it should be used as a springboard to global issues," she says. "And yes, I worry that not all teachers are using it that way."

But we're not making it easy for teachers. Many of those who defend the emphasis on thematic and skills-based teaching argue that its deficiencies boil down to a need for better training, although I personally wonder if this is a slight cop-out: we'd do teachers a tremendous service by offering resources and guidelines to fill the knowledge deficit, and it would help if one teacher in any given year didn't have to guess at what students had studied the year before. It's a problem not only here in Canada, but in other countries, too: a 2007 U.K. Ofsted report complained that school history had become too fragmented, to the effect that students lacked an understanding of basic chronology (one teacher candidate in England told me that she'd heard of a student asking if Churchill and Henry VIII got along well). When that report came out, sales of H.E. Marshall's 1905 children's book *Our Island Story* rocketed. The writing is dated, preachy, and jingoistic, and certainly not an example of good history, but it appealed to parents worried about their children's ignorance of any kind of national timeline.

We face the same challenge here. Social studies are too often taught in a disconnected, uncoordinated fashion, and while historical thinking is rightly emphasized, there's often an incomplete foundation of basic knowledge to support it.

The problem carries into the universities, too. Margaret Macmillan is emeritus professor of international history at Oxford University and a professor of history at the University of Toronto. The bestselling author of *Paris 1919*, she has produced a number of significant works on subjects ranging from women in the Raj to Nixon's historic visit to China (she is also the aunt of popular historian Dan Snow, himself the son of journalists Peter Snow and Ann MacMillan). When we spoke, she was preparing an essay for *Prospect* on the rising popularity of applied history and the need for government departments to be better historically informed.

"We've lost something with the fragmentation of the curriculum," she told me. "Sequence matters. This doesn't mean lists of dates . . . but World War Two wouldn't have been possible without World War One." Back when Macmillan started teaching at Ryerson, she explained, chronology was taught and specialization began in the third and fourth years. Even non-historians "still need to have a good sense of the past," and this requires a more coherent curriculum. "What do we want students to learn? What do we want to teach them? You can have choice, but you also have to be prescriptive. History courses now are devised by the people who want to teach them," hence the prevalence of such niche courses as the history of beer and the history of prostitution at U of T's Scarborough campus, "but it should also be possible to tell faculty what to teach."

Her concerns were echoed by my former tutor, Dr. Gauci, who agrees that we need core requirements as well as options. "I'm struck by how limited the history curriculum in some universities is, and how history now nestles as just another tit-bit within a humanities smorgasbord," he wrote in an email. "Colleagues have said that they feel this has been the result of a 'death by a thousand cuts' over the last thirty years, as student-led demand (as opposed to a faculty strategy) has guided university policy."

As a result, Dr. Gauci fears a three-tier system emerging at university level: one that creates a divide between research-intensive universities "with the libraries and teaching faculty to teach history well"; teaching-only universities, "where history teaching isn't backed up with the same quality of research support"; and universities where history is rolled into a general humanities program.

It's a common problem throughout North America. "Social scientists are failing in their duty and failing the country by retreating to their caves and spending their time grooming each other," Professor Bothwell told me. And this decline in public awareness of the faculty serves to distance academics further from the public. "How many have any public recognition at all? Which feeds into a decline in the standing of the subject generally."

The streaming effect alluded to by Dr. Gauci starts to creep in insidiously early. As we've seen in Ontario, history options in public high schools tend to be chosen by those on an "academic" track, and elementary-aged kids with an interest in history have to make do with a scattergun approach. Historica's education director, Bronwyn Graves, informed me in an email that the organization has plans to make content available for younger students, although currently their materials are geared to support high school courses. Only four of Canada's thirteen provinces and territories mandate the teaching of Canadian history in high school, however (others, according to Historica CEO Anthony Wilson-Smith, "approach equivalency in teaching history under other rubrics," i.e., social sciences, as Lindsay Gibson also pointed out). "It's something we find, frankly, quite frustrating for obvious reasons," Wilson-Smith told me.

It shouldn't be up to an organization such as Historica to pick up the slack in historical content for schools: that's something for education ministries, school boards, and university departments to address. Which is how we find ourselves back where I began this section, with the problem of the divide between historians and curriculum designers, and some fundamental disagreements about how students should learn history.

* * *

Late in 2020, leaked proposals for Alberta's updated elementary social studies curriculum from the United Conservative Party (UCP) caused an uproar in the press and educational circles for their suggestion that residential school history not be taught in the earliest grades, as well as for their inclusion of Biblical passages (to be presented as "sociology/poetry" that could be compared to creation stories from other cultures, not as dogma or doctrine; a detail many reports ignored). In a blog post on her website, Dr. Carla Peck, an Alberta curriculum expert with a background in elementary education, called the document "repulsive, regressive, and grounded in racist ideology that positions White, Western, Christian knowledge as superior to any other knowledge." She continued: "The almost complete omission of Indigenous people, culture, and history in these recommendations is more than symbolic violence. It is erasure."[65]

These are extremely serious and worrying charges and, yet, the "almost complete omission" of Indigenous content still included references to Indigenous art, music, spirituality, hunting practices, trade, tools, and kinship systems. Furthermore, the leaked proposals suggested, among other things, that K-2 students recognize how choices in First Nation, Métis, and Inuit communities contribute to sustainability, and learn about ancestral teachings about respect.

I believe that Indigenous history must be better taught in both the elementary and senior grades, and that public schools should remain free of religious doctrine, but I highlight the controversy to illustrate the strong interpretative bias that quickly came into play around a draft document that had not yet been approved. The draft curriculum, and the process by which it was developed and defended by the Alberta government, has undoubtedly been shown to be seriously flawed (and continues to be a subject of heated debate as this book goes to press). At the same time, some of the more sweeping accusations launched by several of its critics against the third major flashpoint of the leaked proposal, namely, the advice to build up more core historical knowledge in the early grades, also warrant scrutiny.

Dr. Peck's response to the suggestion that students learn certain significant dates and historic events with a view to being able to draw on this knowledge later was uncompromising: "Ok, got it. Understanding is not important," she wrote in another blog post.

It's these sorts of leaps that help to create the totalizing discourses that make balanced discussion difficult. Greg Ashman is a teacher and PhD candidate in Ballarat, Australia, who has authored two books on teaching and is a prolific commentator on education. His response to Dr Peck's claims that knowledge-based history programs dull enthusiasm and understanding is straightforward: it's a straw man. "I would never give someone a cricket rule book and ask them to memorize rules, just like I would never give them a history textbook and ask them to memorise dates and facts,"[66] he tweeted.

Indeed, as Daisy Christodoulou notes in *Seven Myths About Education*, this simplification between knowledge versus understanding isn't helpful. In fact, it's an utterly false dichotomy. While learning the date of the Battle of Waterloo is not in itself useful or meaningful, learning that date in the context of a handful of other dates (as well as a couple of key facts about why each one is important) is extremely useful, as it forms a fundamental chronology that's necessary for all historical understanding. And knowledge has a funny way of begetting more knowledge (my husband came downstairs after reading a chapter about Peter the Great from *The Story of the World* to our then eight-year-old. "I'd never thought about the Sea of Azov until reading this to her tonight," he said, "and then this story about a Russian oil tanker exploding there pops up on my news feed a couple of hours later." Connections happen when you know stuff).

Similarly, Christoloudou writes: "Being a good researcher goes far beyond just being sceptical about what turns up on the first page of a Google search, and depends to a far greater extent on the knowledge you have about the topic being researched."[67] She cites an example from the online edition of the *Guardian*:

> Germany and France have struck a grand bargain that they hope will save the euro, burying their difference over a rigorous new regime to drive down Eurozone debt and restore market confidence in the battered single currency.

This single, small paragraph requires political and geographical background knowledge to understand. Most broadsheet articles assume such knowledge, which has to be acquired somewhere; favouring the teaching of "thinking skills" isn't enough. Other countries appear to realize this: even such culturally disparate nations as Sweden, France, and Japan, for instance, teach a set curriculum of core knowledge in the first six grades.

Still, the skills/knowledge debate seems to be alive and well, despite proponents on both sides recognizing, at least in theory, that you need *both* to do history effectively. It lives on not as a meaningful pedagogical discussion, however, but as a debate of politics. On her blog, Dr. Peck describes E.D. Hirsch's Core Knowledge Foundation as "a conservative educational organization based in the United States that promotes the importance of accumulating background knowledge before students can do anything else."[68]

The problem with slapping a political label on core knowledge is that it's not only baseless (Hirsch has described himself as a lifelong Democrat and "practically a socialist," while core knowledge has been widely embraced by America's second largest teachers' union, the AFT, which has partnered with Britain's National Union of Teachers on a number of progressive initiatives, for years now). It also perpetuates an unnecessary divide between proponents of content mastery and proponents of thinking skills. (As Stanford education professor Sam Wineburg notes, "too often, whether we like someone's politics determines whether we like their history . . . and the question mark falls victim to the exclamation point."[69])

In Hirsch's own words from an interview with left-leaning think tank New America:

> If you really want to be effective in changing power structure or the society, you had better be able to manage that machinery. It's a real paradox that people damned [*Cultural Literacy*], but in doing so demonstrated their own cultural literacy, because they're using allusions that only a

person who is extremely well educated could understand. There is this kind of strange elitism in the reaction of the academic left to *Cultural Literacy*, which is very egalitarian in its impulses.[70]

Dr. Peck's rhetorical attack on core knowledge shows just how oversimplification and polarization of these discussions leads us to miss the bigger point. Skills are a function of background knowledge: without some foundational knowledge, it's impossible to judge new information to discern the truth and reliability of evidence. Elsewhere on her blog, she refers to esteemed Canadian educationalist Professor Ken Osborne without acknowledging that Osborne was also convinced that our concentration on important historical thinking skills has meant a lack of attention to content. Writing in a 2013 edition of the *Journal of the Manitoba Social Science Teachers' Association*, he observed:

> What made the citizens of *Nineteen Eighty-Four* so vulnerable to the lies of Big Brother was not lack of skills but lack of knowledge. Highly skilled technically, their ignorance of the past made it impossible for them to resist Big Brother's manipulation of history. And it is not enough to say that these days all we need to know is how to access some database. We need knowledge in our heads, not simply at our finger-tips.

But doesn't getting knowledge into our heads mean hours of soul-destroying rote memorization? Of course not. Anyone who's interacted with a seven-year-old knows that their brains can hold an unlimited amount of information about Pokémon and *Star Wars*. Most experts agree that knowledge is best attained through meaningful engagement and active learning. Suggesting that mastering half a dozen dates over the course of an academic year is somehow going to dampen children's enthusiasm for learning does a great disservice to the ability of teachers to make learning fun, as well as to children's natural curiosity and delight in the power that knowledge brings.

(I wrote twice to Dr. Peck to ask for her thoughts on all of these points, but I never received a reply. She is currently leading a seven-year, pan-Canadian study called Thinking Historically for Canada's Future, designed to understand the current state of history education in Canada: the first of its kind since 1968. The study will include an examination of K-12 history curriculum and resources, as well as teaching and learning practices. It will be fascinating to follow its progress and see what conclusions it produces.)

"Edu-Twitter" can be a font of inspiring discussion and idea sharing, but when it comes to talking curriculum, many threads may leave the impartial observer wondering whether it's really the adults standing at the front of the classroom. There's swagger, trolling, and a surprising amount of qualification-quoting: a form of juvenile posturing that also manifests in trading in passive-aggressive GIFs when debates devolve. The most over-inflated egos and shrillest protestations tend to come from the extremes, and Twitter is an echo chamber *par excellence* for extremes and false dichotomies. It's a bit like my kids' karaoke microphone, which amplifies and warps sounds in a way that's highly entertaining but nevertheless distorted. It's sad to think that the discourse around learning has, as in so many arenas, become intensely polarized and politicized. Neither side is really listening to the other. It's also misleading: certain sections of pedagogical Twitter are better organized and more social-media savvy than others, which means that highly coordinated Twitter-storms can create the impression of a vast movement that's not necessarily so large or united in real life.

One such movement likes to claim that core knowledge promotes sage-on-the-stage, instructivist teaching, despite the fact that neither E.D. Hirsch nor the CKF advises on pedagogy. Plenty of pedagogical research does, however, support knowledge-rich learning. Daniel Willingham is an acclaimed cognitive scientist and professor at the University of Virginia, who distilled decades of research into easily digestible conclusions in his recently re-issued book *Why Don't Students Like School? A Cognitive Scientist Answers Questions About How the Mind Works and What It Means For the Classroom.* "Data from the last thirty years leads to a conclusion that is not scientifically challengeable: thinking well requires knowing facts, and that's true not simply because you need something to think *about*," he writes. "The very processes that teachers care most about–critical thinking processes such as reasoning and problem solving–are intimately intertwined with factual knowledge that is stored in long-term memory."[71]

He cites as an example a class of middle school students that read a story describing an inning of a baseball game. Half were good readers, and half were weak readers. When it came to answering questions about the story, the ones who performed best were the ones who knew a lot about baseball, not necessarily the ones who were good readers. In other words, what the students *knew* mattered more than how skilled they were at reading.

Obviously, we have to be selective about what knowledge we consider important, because there isn't time to learn absolutely everything. For that reason, Willingham suggests, we should focus on learning the concepts that recur frequently: put that knowledge in place, he advises, so it's there for critical thinking to happen. Recognize that shallow knowledge is better than no knowledge, and that some kids won't be getting it at home while others will, which is why it's one role of schools to help level the playing field by making sure that all students can draw on a common knowledge. Deep knowledge may take more time to develop, because it has to be richly interconnected. That's why knowledge has to be built up cumulatively, allowing students time to digest smaller pieces before connecting them to a larger whole.

Susan Wise Bauer echoes this wisdom in *The Well-Trained Mind*. "Critical thinking can't be taught in isolation," she writes:

> You can't teach a child to follow a recipe without actually providing butter, sugar, flour, and salt; piano skills can't be

taught without a keyboard . . . A math student can't think critically about how to find the area of a triangle unless she already knows the formula for finding the area of a square. A fifth grader can't analyze the fall of Rome until she knows the facts about Rome's decay.

Knowledge continues to build as we grow; just because middle school students have outgrown the sponge phase of learning doesn't mean that they suddenly stop absorbing new information. "Instead of passively accepting this information," Bauer explains, they will "be interacting with it–deciding on its value, its purpose, and its place in the scheme of knowledge."[72]

Discovery learning (also known as inquiry learning, a pedagogy devised in the 1960s in which students use their own experiences, hands-on experimentation, intuition, and creativity to uncover facts and information) has all sorts of benefits, particularly in terms of getting students engaged; but, Willingham writes, there's evidence that the brain retains as much about incorrect "discoveries" as about correct ones. This means teachers have more work to do to keep students on track to think deeply about meaning. He also calls into question another popular trend of teaching students to "think like experts": one which appears to promise exciting engagement with a subject but overlooks the fact that "no one thinks like a scientist or a historian without a great deal of training." Professional historians think like expert historians because they have years and years of knowledge behind them. You can't replicate that in a class that's encountering a topic for the first time. "It's not just that students know less than experts; it's also that what they know is organized differently in their memory,"[73] Willingham says.

It is fun to do science experiments in high school, and these experiences help students to retain information and grow curiosity; but the standard pattern of being taught a lesson, then doing a lab to "prove" the lesson, is obviously not how real science works. (In my first year studying history as an undergraduate at Oxford, we mainly constructed arguments in essays and tutorials based on what other historians had written. Analyzing sources deeply came later, in the further and special subjects. Considered from this perspective, expecting elementary students to learn history mainly through "hands-on" primary source analysis doesn't quite stack up.) Understanding generally comes before creation, and experts create because they not only understand their field, they also add new knowledge to it. "A more modest and realistic goal for students is knowledge comprehension," writes Willingham. "A student may not be able to write a new narrative of historical fact, but she can follow and understand different accounts of [e.g.,] the Constitutional Convention as a way of learning how historians develop narratives."[74]

As became clear in my conversation with Lindsay Gibson, there's a similar tension at work between teaching history and practising it. University of Toronto professor Ruth Sandwell recalls in her article "History is a Verb: Teaching Historical Practise to Teacher Education Students,"[75] that as a historian she "was actively engaged in creating history as a process of knowing," whereas as a teacher, "I dispensed history as a product to be passively consumed." But instead of seeing these things in opposition, Sandwell seems to suggest that a degree of knowledge-building is a necessary first step before meaningful historical thinking can happen. She points out, for instance, that elementary children need vast guidance in identifying and selecting primary documents, let alone analyzing them, even before they start to build meaningful historical arguments. She quotes another researcher who observed that "each student had an opinion, and they were eager to share. But none of the [students'] opinions had any relationship to the evidence that they had just spent three days evaluating." Sandwell notes in her conclusion that teachers are up against a "disdain for disciplinary knowledge, especially in the case of history, in the public school system," and so the same roundabout methods of instruction persist.

The result, as Trish McMahon has seen with her elder son, is that "themes and micro histories dominate, with a definite focus on what could be called social history and not political history." McMahon believes that it's vital for historians to research and students to learn about the stories of those who have for too long been excluded from grand narratives; but in the process, she told me, "historical study came to be studies about perspective." Once everyone's perspective is considered valid, the shift from "perspective" to "facts" renders facts a social construct. "You can see where this ends up by looking at the news and current events," she said. "There are no longer facts but 'facts' and 'alternative facts.' Without a solid grounding in history, people don't have the basic general knowledge to understand the world around them. Conviction becomes a substitute for accuracy."

Conviction has come to play a major role in school history teaching today, particularly among educators and curriculum specialists who take an activist historical approach. One such advisor, Samantha Cutrara, is an education strategist at York University. She writes on her website:

> If you've followed my work . . . you may know my purpose of teaching history is to TRANSFORM—make the world a better place because of the stories and ideas we learn from the past. These two things are inextricably interwoven because when you know history, especially the histories that have been marginalized, you WANT to change the world with the stories of resistance, resilience, and survival. Because, if you're not doing history to make change, then what the f*** are you doing it for? As was the case before this moment, this will continue to be the main thrust of my work moving into the future.[76]

The author is keen to examine assumptions not only about student knowledge, but what knowledge means for teachers: "Research has shown, including my own, that teachers, especially history teachers, like to teach from a place of knowledge and comfort. This is normal—you want to know what you are going to teach and don't want to be put on the spot. However, we are limited in what we know. And we are limited in how we can teach and share stories that are different than, even challenge, our own."[77] (Such ambivalence reminded me of another Dr Gauci observation. "I am a little cautious when I hear that tutors declare themselves to be 'facilitators' rather than teachers," he admitted. "As one of my students once said, 'I want my professors to know their stuff!'")

Cutrara goes farther in her critique of historical thinking, which she argues "imposes a settler grammar over the study of the past in such ways that widens the gulf between Aboriginal and Euro-Canadian knowledge systems, lessening the space available to develop the respect, openness for truth, and room for relationality needed to develop relationships of reconciliation." Historical thinking, she continues, "has an intolerance for the type of work needed to decolonize history education and Indigenize our understanding of the Canadian past."[78]

Having looked more closely into Cutrara's work—her first book, *Transforming the Canadian History Classroom: Imagining a New 'We'*, came out in 2020—I found myself agreeing with some of this argument, largely because it leaves some room for oral traditions, personal connections, and (here I go again!) "story." Ditto her critique of addressing representation through the "cliché" of "just add more Black history to the curriculum and stir" without providing for meaningful complexity.

I'm less certain about some of what she writes about privileging student interest and downplaying teacher expertise ("Students have so much of the world's knowledge on their phones that a teacher's role in the classroom should not be that of expert but as one who facilitates students' learning by telling a story that students can add to themselves.") This falls squarely into the realm of "learnification" (a term coined by education research professor Gert Biesta): a popular pedagogical trend that, according to critics such as Paul Bennett, "promulgated by ministries of education and education faculties, [subverts] the real point of education—to learn *something*, to learn it *for a reason*, and to learn it *from someone*."[79]

Cutrara's stress on engaging student interest by presenting active invitations to students to "connect information to their prior knowledge" makes excellent sense if we also acknowledge that some prior knowledge has to exist. For this reason, some educators might question the proposal of teaching through "historic space": having students pick out key terms from their textbook to create a mind map of a topic *before* filling in the content to make meaningful connections (thereby challenging the master narrative with "counterstories") sounds like a potentially rewarding exercise that could nevertheless also result in piecemeal understanding.

The emphasis on "transforming" in the above blurb is perhaps misleading. It's possible to read transformation as being part of a teacher's job in the broadest sense: a good teacher will transform a student's way of seeing the world. Cutrara's call for a holistic and inclusive approach to teaching is sincere and extremely worthwhile, as are her arguments for the importance of connection and care in the classroom.

The problem, as Patrice Dutil notes in his April 2021 review of Cutrara's book in the *Literary Review of Canada*, is that what she's really talking about isn't history, but social studies for the speaking-my-truth generation. Dutil, an author and professor of politics at Ryerson University (he also founded the *LRC* back in 1991), despairs that:

> [l]ike many people who teach in faculties of education—and who write provincial curriculum guidelines—Cutrara has a particularly narrow view of the discipline. And while she calls for a "transformation" of the subject, she is evidently unfazed by the fact that only three provinces—Ontario, Quebec, and Manitoba—currently require a course in Canadian history for high school students to graduate . . .
>
> And that's what makes this book important: it contributes yet another argument for knowing less about our country. This is what passes as "thinking about history" in today's faculties of education—maybe even in some classrooms. Cutrara is on a mission, and it is not about teaching students about the past.

What, then, is her mission? Cutrara's focus is not on the discipline of history so much as on "the collective identities of the present classroom." As Dutil explains:

> To be *meaningful* (her emphasis), history must bolster the student's sense of self. This can be done only if students *see*

themselves in the lesson plan. Cutrara sees her proposed transformation as part of a broader mission of Indigenizing and decolonizing Canadian culture.

There is nothing wrong with this mission: teachers have to know their students in order to teach them effectively, and addressing entrenched structural barriers to equitable learning is a necessary cause. But these are separate issues from how to teach the particular and peculiar subject of history, and the distinction isn't one that Cutrara and many other curriculum design experts are prepared to acknowledge. In Dutil's words, "she comes at the discipline not from a historical perspective, but from one of 'critical theory' and 'critical pedagogy.' Because Canadian history is 'so messy, so complicated, so violent' (compared with what, I ask?), she believes it can be taught only through critical race theory, feminist theory, and post-structuralism."

"These are the faculties that hold power over the curricula," Dutil concludes. "And that stranglehold—supported by governments of left and right—must be challenged. Otherwise, the result will be a society that is awesomely ignorant of its own history, not to mention the history of the world."

As one letter writer observed in a later issue of the *LRC*, "by rushing too quickly to 'mobilize' history, to create the world she desires, [Cutrara] seems not to have understood the history she wants to mobilize, nor the world she wants to change."[80]

There's a fundamental problem with any approach that assumes we need to "use" history. As Sam Wineburg writes, "in viewing the past as usable, something that speaks to us without intermediary or translation, we end up turning it into yet another commodity for instant consumption. We discard or just ignore vast regions of the past that either contradict our current needs or fail to align tidily with them."[81] We've got to be prepared to embrace the contradictions, foreignness and discomfort of the past:

> The narcissist sees the world—both the past and the present—in his own image. Mature historical knowing teaches us to do the opposite: to go beyond our own image, to go beyond our brief life, and to go beyond the fleeting moment in human history into which we have been born. History educates ("leads outward" in the Latin) in the deepest sense. Of the subjects in the secular curriculum, it is the best at teaching those virtues once reserved for theology— humility in the face of our limited ability to know, and awe in the face of the expanse of human history.[82]

The impetus to use the study of history to make change is something that appears to come much more from educators and curriculum specialists rather than from historians themselves. Indeed, when I put this to Margaret Macmillan, she expressed a concern that "the pendulum has swung too far: my purpose is not to teach my students to demand social justice [but] to try to understand the past, and to understand the present." Here she echoes the guiding ambition of one of the discipline's founders,

Leopold von Ranke, who wrote in 1824 of his desire not to instruct future generations but only to describe "how it really was." Ranke was well aware of the problem of impartiality, but his desire to capture as much truth as possible, as objectively as possible, remains the goal of all good historians today. (That's not to say that historians write without passion or commitment. As Lynn Hunt notes, "The truest history is often written by people with deep commitments on one side or other of an issue. Blandness is not the same thing as truth."[83])

Remember that school friend of mine for whom the Heritage Minutes were her first glimpse of diversity in Canadian history? Her name is Ruta. The daughter of members of the South Asian diaspora who fled Idi Amin's Uganda in the 1970s, Ruta is Oxford- and Yale-educated and now a co-founder of a migration-focused consultancy firm. I asked her about her thoughts on the shift to a change-making or activist narrative among history educators. Ruta is neither a teacher nor an historian, but she is someone who conducts research with the aim of influencing policy decisions that can mean the difference between life and death for thousands in some of the world's most troubled areas.

"If you teach critical thinking and sympathy together, I think you engender change," she reflected. "If you just teach change-making, I think you end up, as a society, with black squares on Instagram but no one volunteering at inner-city schools, [in other words, with] a system in which it's easy to virtue signal, and few people recognize the importance of analyzing results."

She went on to make an observation that resonated with me: "The thing that worries me about the 'making kids into change-makers' approach is that, honestly, not everyone is a change-maker. And to some degree, not everyone should be." Change for the sake of change can be counterproductive, and meaningful change also comes in different forms. "If you're going to make kids into change-makers, you also need to help them analyze what kinds of changes they will propose."

As one of the most thoughtful people I know—a voracious and ambitious reader who got her start as a child devouring Greek and Norse mythology in the Mississauga public library— Ruta's take on engaging students while also informing them was of interest to me. She felt that her own school experience didn't deliver on the broad overview: "It would have been handy to have been taught some kind of clear trajectory—to have spent one foundation year, at some point, being taught what happened when." But she does recall that "interactive activities . . . made me think, and if you do simulations, [students] have the chance to see the sides of both [e.g.] the colonizers and the colonized. It becomes less about inclusion, and more about critical thinking."

"Teaching history through the lens of the historical thinking concepts can reinforce the need for an evidence-based approach to evaluation of past and present events," Christina Ganev wrote to me, echoing this take. But there's more to the study of history than the interpretation of evidence: there's also a need for historical knowledge and awareness of causation and context, and the ability to look for big patterns (while recognizing that the "story" of history changes with each new generation). I would argue that, by emphasizing present-day applications of historical skills, we sometimes risk losing sight of the other things that history teaches—humility and skepticism as well as pride and a sense of wonder—and what distinguishes it from other subjects.

"In a world of disinformation (or simply information overload) . . . I am evermore struck by the cultural values which the humanities impart (as opposed to the focus on skills)," Dr. Gauci reflected. I would humbly suggest that such values are passed down to students not only through lessons in critical thinking, but also in cultural capital: the knowledge—diverse, global, and multi-layered—that's required to understand what we read in the newspaper or scroll through on social media. Just because that knowledge doesn't always have obviously or immediately practical ends doesn't make it any less valuable.

"Is the *Epic of Gilgamesh* relevant to students in a way that they can understand right now?" Willingham writes. "If I'm continually trying to build bridges between students' daily lives and their school subjects, the students may get the message that school is always about them, whereas I think there is value, interest, and beauty in learning things that don't have much to do with me."[84]

Students themselves seem to align with this: of the group I surveyed in 2020, less than 30 per cent said that they were primarily interested in history as it related directly to them and their communities. Curiosity is an opportunity to be embraced.

It's also a plea from our youth that we have a responsibility to heed and address (the Greek poet Menander perhaps knew this when he wrote, in the third century BCE: "In many ways, the saying "know thyself" is not well said. It is more practical to say "know other people!"). While children from privileged families and communities may be spoilt with opportunities for enriched encounters with the world beyond their immediate environs and experiences, this isn't true across the board.

Natalie Wexler asked in the August 2019 issue of *Atlantic*,

> What if the medicine we have been prescribing is only making matters worse, particularly for poor children? What if the best [approach] is not to drill kids on discrete skills but to teach them, as early as possible, the very things we've marginalized—including history, science, and other content that could build the knowledge and vocabulary they need to understand both written texts and the world around them? As the years go by, children of educated parents continue to acquire more knowledge and vocabulary outside school, making it easier for them to gain even more knowledge— because, like Velcro, knowledge sticks best to other, related knowledge.

The problem, again, appears to boil down to conflicting messaging. "Many teachers have told me that they'd like to spend more time on social studies and science, because their students clearly enjoy learning actual content," Wexler continued:

But they've been informed that teaching skills is *the* way to boost reading comprehension. Education policy makers and reformers have generally not questioned this approach and in fact, by elevating the importance of reading scores, have intensified it . . . [But] if students lack the knowledge and vocabulary to understand the passages on reading tests, they won't have an opportunity to demonstrate their skill in making inferences or finding the main idea. And if they arrive at high school without having been exposed to history or science, as is the case for many students from low-income families, they won't be able to read and understand high-school-level materials.[85]

It may seem impossible to steer a course between so many apparently conflicting ideologies, but as the next chapter will show, there are several success stories from which we can draw inspiration.

III

WHAT CAN BE DONE

Success stories

D ANUTA KEAN WAS IN her forties when she decided to leave a successful career in journalism to retrain as a high school history teacher. I'd written reviews for her when she worked as a magazine books editor, and when I heard about her decision to change professions, I was eager to know more. Given the challenges and stresses of school teaching, and the various raging controversies around history teaching in Britain today, I was curious to find out why it seemed like an attractive move.

Danuta told me that she'd grown increasingly frustrated with journalism, a not uncommon complaint, and felt, after a good run that included producing five reports on diversity, as well as writing and editing the *Guardian*'s books website, that she wanted to move to help support a younger generation facing an increasingly unpredictable world. Furthermore, as she saw it, the move to teaching history was actually an outgrowth of something she'd been nurturing all along: a love for story.

The first in her family to do A-levels, let alone go to university, Danuta loved history and writing from the start. "I was obsessed with non-fiction accounts of history at a very young age," she told me. "I remember being fascinated by pictures of Charles I on the scaffold with his head cut off. This sounds gory, but I wanted to understand where that brutality came from and how we respond to it." (I suspect most writers and historians could draw on a similar moment: I can certainly vividly recall being fascinated, at age seven, by a colourized engraving of a *gendarme* holding up the bloody head of Louis XVI).

History was also something Danuta related to on a personal level. "My mother's family was Irish Catholic, and storytelling about ancestors is fundamental to their culture. I believe one of the failures of the history curriculum has been to not engage with children from broader cultural backgrounds and to capitalize on the oral storytelling tradition many of us grew up in."

All humans share an instinct for storytelling, as well as a need for joined-up narratives that help us make sense of the world. Cognitive scientist Jerome Bruner described two ways of knowing—paradigmatic and narrative—the second of which draws on emotion to strengthen the power of memory. Stories engage our feelings, which makes us interested in a subject; but they also give shape to information, which helps us develop understanding.

The most effective stories aren't just about feelings, however. As an award-winning journalist and journalism instructor,

Danuta says, "I've noticed a real difference in those who have an Eng Lit degree and those with History degrees. The former tend to care more about the writing and aren't [necessarily as] good at the research and challenging underlying assumptions."

It's this passion for telling stories well—and for interrogating the stories we're told on a daily basis—that informs the most innovative and engaging approaches to teaching history today.

In 2008, Bill Gates happened upon a collection of talks by Australian professor Dr. David Christian, released as part of the Teaching Company's Big Courses DVD series. Dr Christian's *Big History* talks aimed to explain fourteen billion years of history, from the Big Bang to the present day, in a single course by combining history, biology, astronomy, and various other fields. His idea of "one big, cosmic story" and "the underlying unity of modern knowledge," itself inspired by the work of early twentieth-century French historians who argued that history is best understood by scale switching through time and space, caught Gates's attention. He soon became committed to making the course available not only to university students but high-school kids, as well. Gates and Christian reached out to Professor Bob Bain, an award-winning associate professor at the University of Michigan (Ann Arbor) with joint appointments in the history, education, and museum studies departments, to help develop the curriculum and assessment for such a course, which would eventually become known as the Big History Project (BHP). It piloted in five schools in 2011 and more than doubled in each of its first three years; by 2014, 1,200 schools were offering it.

Today, the BHP continues to be included as an elective at thousands of schools across the United States and globally (while Dr. Christian's TED Talk, "The History of Our World in 18 Minutes," has had twelve million views to date). It remains totally free, flexible, and comprehensive, and can be adapted for instruction in the elementary, middle or high school years. It's not a replacement for traditional history courses, which promote specialized focus on historical methodology and detail, but as a synthesizing overview that draws connections between subjects, it's a worthy orientation vehicle.

It has also now been around long enough to have demonstrated a significant improvement in both student writing and thinking skills. "Everyone is attracted by the scale of it," Bain told me, "but it's actually the spiralling sets of pedagogical activities which lie beneath the surface" that develop the real skills: the course offers ten investigations centred on document-based questions that connect kids' natural curiosity to the content they have to master.

"It's not just about memorizing someone else's narrative, but also learning how to interpret narratives; they're constantly asked how to support claims," he explained. Yes, it's arranged around a large framework that organizes huge movements through time and, yes, there's a justified suspicion of "master" narratives being taught as unquestioned truth in schools today, "but we *want* kids to critique it," Bain said.

"We've seen evidence that students have ended up with knowledge in fragments," he continued, the result of "any (BHP)

coherent narrative on either side [of the political divide]—
history as a glory story *or* a horror story" dissipating over the last
decade. There are inherent dangers to any simplified narrative,
Bain says, but that doesn't change the fact that "stories help
orient us to the present, and if you've got no story, then you're
primed for someone else to give one to you."

"If I take my three-year-old granddaughter to a birthday
party, I'll explain what the story will be," he offered, by way of
example. There will be games, singing, and cake, maybe even
party bags. Anticipation and interest heightens and we now
know broadly what to expect. That doesn't mean that the story
will always be the same, of course. Bain has since moved on to
a new course, The World History Project (WHP), which "tacks
back and forth between the big narrative and details, asking, 'do
the details support, extend, or challenge the larger framework?'"

Now in the second year of the WHP pilot, Bain predicts that
it will have an even bigger effect than the BHP. "It's a text-heavy
course, and the texts have to be offered at four different levels
so that no matter where students are, they can engage with it."
This kind of narrative-based thinking can start with very young
students, Bain says ("You can ask a kindergartener to tell 'Jack
and the Beanstalk' from the point of view of the giant") and
has had proven success with middle and late elementary-aged
students, in particular.

We know that stories are psychologically privileged; we also
know that they share the same fundamental ingredients as any
good history, or what Willingham calls "the four Cs": causality,

conflict, character, and complications. Stories may be easy to remember, but that doesn't have to mean that they're simple: they require the power of inference to interpret them meaningfully, and they can easily be turned around to reveal different truths (we can explain the American entry into the Second World War through the bombing of Pearl Harbour, or we can consider the Japanese attack from the Japanese perspective, taking into account Imperial Japan's goals and perceived obstacles to those goals). They also provide a launch point for us to ask important questions.

"Sixteen per cent of the Polish population died during World War II," Bain reflected. "We can ask students, 'What do you imagine would happen to a country in these circumstances?'" By learning to form hypotheses based on evidence, as well as acknowledging contingencies, we remember that history isn't inevitable, that people have agency, and that the story can always change. We learn to read history forward, by considering the consequences of actions, not by projecting what we know of the present *back* onto the past, and then we can start to anticipate what might happen next.

"Let's take narrative seriously," says Bain. "Let's identify ones which have no credibility, like Holocaust denial, then let's ask students, 'What are the different ways of telling a story, and what's the evidence? What are the consequences of accepting one over the other?'" Every narrative will have its limitations, flaws, and biases, but having a big picture is "cognitively critical" to understanding the past. Approaching history with no knowledge of a larger story, according to Bain, is a bit like trying to complete a 1,000-piece puzzle without the box-top picture to help as a guide.

There have always been those who would critique "total history," the sort of broad, cross-curricular syntheses of the past most recently popularized by such writers as Yuval Noah Harari, bestselling author of *Sapiens, Homo Deus: A Brief History of Tomorrow*, and *21 Lessons for the 21st Century*. "There's obviously a taste for it," Margaret Macmillan acknowledged when I asked for her take on "big history" movements, although she advised a degree of caution in such an approach: "The trouble is it can all become a great big porridge and people can't locate themselves in it." Obviously, such courses can't be exhaustive and they shouldn't replace approaches to learning local, national, or period-specific histories. But as a way of framing more detailed study, they offer an engaging framework that can make history meaningful to students.

Educators elsewhere are innovating similar strategies that also prioritize story: "Reading Like a Historian" is one project that has come out of Stanford and is aimed at K-12 students, while "Reacting to the Past" (developed by Mark Carnes at Barnard College) uses role-playing games to place students quite literally *in* the story.

What's the story? It's the first question any editor will ask a writer; it also happens to be the question that Dr. Perry Gauci asks his students to keep in mind as they prepare for finals. There need to be bookends, an arc, a cycle, a narrative: only then can we analyse and identify motives and key elements. And yes, there is always a multiplicity of stories. "Historians do two things: we measure, and we explain," said Dr. Gauci, and that applies not just to the minutiae of history, but to the layers of narratives that make up the subject. "Where in the trench does that story lie? What stories overlay it?" Growing up as the grandson of Maltese immigrants living on the Welsh border, a young Perry grew accustomed to asking these questions to understand "the structures in which my life was organized," and it is these questions that continue to guide his research and teaching today.

If we can agree that history truly is, in the words of Bob Davis, "not a few techniques to acquire but a passionate story to be learned, a story with lessons for the present," then the challenges of clearly discerning bias in narrative techniques and structure shouldn't cause us to throw out story itself. In our eagerness to dissect and deconstruct master narratives, crucial and worthwhile though this process may be, we've perhaps forgotten the value of story to bring us together—and, for our youngest learners, to engage them with the past in the first place.

"Unravelling the deep biases of the traditional canon MUST be undertaken,"[86] Davis wrote. "But now the unravelling process has been stopped since the 'knitting classes,' the connecting of stories into a larger narrative pattern, have been cancelled. I need to stress my commitment to the necessity of this unravelling process since it is customary to consider defenders of 'totalizing discourses' to be conservatives." Indeed, Davis poured his full energy into "an admittedly fragmented situation" by developing

Black history courses that were ground breaking for their time. Drawing inspiration from the great African American historian Nathan Huggins, who argued that Black history has to resist the potential isolation of Black Studies and instead be exploded into the traditional American master narrative, Davis argued: "from these particular histories we should develop new general histories of our country and the world."

This is where we stand today. Rote memorization of disconnected knowledge does not a story make, but neither does an approach that focuses on *deconstructing* narratives before any common knowledge of those stories has been established in the first place. Story has a vital role to play in the very earliest years, and it has an equally vital, if different, function as students become more established in their knowledge and sophisticated in their thinking. Nowadays, there's a fashionable pessimism to downplaying the achievements and worth of liberal democracy: but the fact is that, in many ways, it's the best system we've got and, regardless, it's the world we inhabit. It's worth making sure that we understand it.

As Historica's Anthony Wilson-Smith put it to me, "A good story, meaning one well-told, whether happy or not, is crucial to awakening and holding interest. When historians tell stories well and give us a sense of the people involved, we can empathize and understand. It would be a tragedy and a waste if, for example, young people didn't learn about Canada's role in two world wars, and aspects such as the heroism of Canadians then; the sacrifices; the ways in which we still feel the effects today." He continued:

My own view, having worked as a journalist in more than thirty-five countries, is that this is certainly one of the best places in the world, but it can and should always strive to get better. There's no arguing, for example, the abysmal treatment of Indigenous peoples and Black Canadians, and we shouldn't try to push that under a carpet out of sight. Ideally, to me, we need a combination of qualities: justified pride in all the great things we have accomplished in our past and continue to achieve, measured with an awareness that there have been many mistakes along the way, and that continues to be the case. Acknowledging both sides is how we continue to get better.

So, if the story is to continue *expanding*, as opposed to fragmenting, where do we begin telling it? And how on earth do we find the time to cover it all?

* * *

One compelling argument is to "go big" from the start. Various highly successful precedents exist for this approach, including the school of thought often described as "classical" education. Here, history is both integrated across subjects and acts as a central pillar that supports learning in all disciplines. For teachers and schools that follow the *trivium*, the three-stage learning process advanced in Plato's dialogues, which progresses from the nuts and bolts of things or "grammar" stage, through the learning-to-interpret or "logic" stage, and culminating in the argument-refining or "rhetoric" stage, history is taught in three four-year cycles, with each cycle delving deeper into a given time period as students' thinking skills develop and mature. So, first graders learn about ancient history, second graders learn about the Middle Ages, third graders learn about early modern times, and fourth graders learn about the modern age; then, in the fifth grade, student return to the beginning, but this time in their study of ancient times they move beyond myths and overviews of ancient life to engage with defining moments in major ancient civilizations. By the time students return to study ancient history for the third and final cycle in the ninth grade, they've reached the stage of being able to re-examine the stories they first heard from a teacher as first graders—possibly, by now, as readers of rudimentary Latin or Greek—with a greater understanding of context and a better ability to explore more complicated subject matter critically.

Not only does this approach have the advantage of allowing students to start broad before going deep, thereby providing a solid foundation of the "big picture" before engaging with analytical and persuasive work in accordance with their developing abilities, it also provides an abundantly rational roadmap for teachers. If everyone worked to a broadly similar program, we'd eliminate the mind-numbing, time-wasting, and completely unnecessary repetition that occurs too frequently in the early years of learning. Furthermore, we'd be offering a curriculum that connects students' learning meaningfully to other subjects. Because each historical period correlates with major scientific advances of the time, students begin with the study of Earth and space in the first grade, then the human body and natural life in the second grade, simple chemistry in the third, and physics (corresponding with the atomic age) in the fourth. The same cyclical approach continues to apply after that, with more advanced study of space, Earth sciences, chemistry, and physics in middle and high school.

Susan Wise Bauer is the author of the four-part *Story of the World* series and the powerhouse behind the massively popular *Well-Trained Mind* books and homeschooling curriculum, which is perhaps the best-known classical education program in North America. She has taught history at both the college and high-school level and offers programs in self-education for adults keen to broaden and deepen their understanding of literature, history, and politics. As an historian and teacher, she is the first to recognize that there is no such thing as a completely unbiased history: medieval historical writing framed the past as part of God's unfolding plan, while later Providential, Whiggish, and Marxist histories all imposed their own filters on history. As a result, all of these, she argues, should be avoided when teaching young children. This means sticking to the classical (Greek) approach of focusing on major actions and events in the earliest years; in other words, focusing on telling a story.

"A mind stocked with the lives of great men and women (and details about the lives of not-so-great ones) is a mind ready to think: ready to understand, in John Arnold's words, that history is an argument."[87] Bauer's logic echoes that of E.D. Hirsch in its celebration of knowledge, even as it promotes more specifically the framing power of *historical* knowledge. Rote memorization of disjointed facts this is not: *connecting* and *deepening* understanding is the very point of the classical approach.

I started reading the first volume of *Story of the World* with my daughter when she was five. We'd take perhaps twenty minutes to half an hour to go through one or two chapters, with me reading aloud and my daughter drawing illustrations of what she heard and whatever captured her interest. We would stop to debate the virtues of several of Hammurabi's more brutal laws, marvel at how one tiny silk worm changed the course of Chinese history, and weigh up the relative achievements of Hatshepsut and Cleopatra. At dinnertime, she would want to clarify the rules around gladiatorial combat and wonder aloud why Spartan women had more rights than women elsewhere in Greece.

At one point, when she became obsessed with the wives of Henry VIII (particularly Catherine Howard), we took a pause between books and she duly dove into her own reading for a while. By the time we reached the second volume, we'd ask her to write a caption for each of her illustrations: one simple takeaway from the story she'd just heard. By volume three, these might range from "No fish! Lewis and Clark stuck in the Rocky Mountains" to "Ferdinand VII and Simon Bolivar play tennis." As we neared the end of the series (she was eight by this point), we could have asked her to write a brief response to each chapter (this is the advice for homeschooling families); but because she liked to listen to *Story of the World* at bedtime, we didn't try to turn it into anything resembling work. Instead, she would draw as she listened, and the conversations that followed spoke of a genuine engagement with what she was absorbing quite distinct from any attempts to postpone bedtime by a few more minutes.

Our daughter is now almost ten and continues to greedily consume books on historical themes, generally without interference from us. I worry that her natural enthusiasm will be tempered by the repetitive, fiercely local, and myopic tenor of social studies classes to come, but I'm also hopeful. Some Canadian schools have already recognized the vital importance of the historical context of knowledge. Toronto's Abelard School, for instance, where graduates consistently gain admission to their top choices of world-class universities across the globe, often on scholarships, describes its curriculum as following "a study of the sciences, mathematics, literature, history, philosophy, and political ideologies in the context of each of the following periods: the Ancient World, the Middle Ages, the Renaissance and Reformation, and the Age of Reason." Tellingly, Abelard is a school founded by teachers. Its philosophy is based on an appreciation of the transformative power of knowledge and a belief in the joy of learning. Of course, many would argue that independent schools such as Abelard enjoy a degree of autonomy and flexibility not often associated with public schools; but I would note that its guiding philosophy is not shaped by lavish resources, exclusive membership, or a restrictive religious, cultural, or political ideology: in other words, there's no reason that its approach not be emulated in any other school, regardless of size, location, or student body.

I also draw immense encouragement from the curiosity of young people themselves. When I taught European history to Grade Twelves in downtown Toronto, even the most reluctant learners couldn't resist getting drawn into the mock trials we held for Robespierre and Louis XVI or our simulation of an Enlightenment *salon* (the macarons may also have been a draw). A young military buff who took a fairly laissez-faire approach to most assignments raised the bar for everyone with a passionate presentation on the German experience at Stalingrad, while the kid who never got off his phone was able to provide a surprisingly eloquent account of what medieval cartography and Google Maps can tell us about pre-modern versus post-modern worldviews. They reflected on Montaigne's "Cannibals" (teenagers are great on what it's like to be an outsider) and Nietzsche (ditto nihilism), reconsidered the Holocaust through narratives of Jewish resistance, and produced a hilarious skit narrated by a diamante-encrusted floozy named Manifest Destiny. Conspiracies were always guaranteed to engage, from the plot to kill Rasputin to Cold War political shenanigans. We even ventured beyond Europe's borders into the Ottoman Empire, where we brushed up against Wahhabism and the roots of the Israel-Palestine conflict, and examined and challenged calls for an Islamic "Reformation."

Perhaps the biggest learning curve for them was striking a balance between style and substance when it came to writing (or, indeed, presenting) on historical topics. Most were very good at questioning, challenging, and critiquing other narratives—this was something that had been instilled at their previous middle and high schools—but they weren't always strong on building a convincing argument of their own with facts to back it up. In other words, they were great at being critical, but not always at thinking critically. (Peter Seixas and Penney Clark touch on a similar challenge in "Obsolete Icons and the Teaching of History," where they describe the challenges of discussing the controversy around George Southwell's murals in the B.C. Parliament Buildings without adequate knowledge about the colonial era: "Though some of the students made claims about the 'accuracy' of the painting, they generally did not get far with these arguments, because they had only the most generic sense of the history of the colonial era that the paintings depicted."[88]) They were also quick to dismiss sources as "biased" without allowing room for different perspectives; this tied into the ongoing project of learning how to build an argument while also recognizing the value of counter arguments.

In other words, to use the classical education terms, my students had leapfrogged over the fact-learning grammar stage, dabbled a bit in the skill-centred logic stage, and landed in the ideas-heavy rhetoric stage, where they often floundered despite their eagerness to revel in big ideas because their knowledge was limited and their skills only half-developed. As a result, we spent as much time mastering facts and practising critical thinking as we did "playing" with the big questions.

My students would groan when I made them write gobbets, miniature primary source exercises I'd been subjected to as an undergraduate (a brief section of text is provided with little to no contextual information, and students must write a paragraph that summarizes, analyzes, and judges it based on what they *do* know), but some of their clearest thinking emerged in those little four-line paragraphs.

They learnt a lot, as did I. But perhaps the biggest takeaway was a bittersweet realization that all we had covered needn't have waited until an optional course at the very end of their school career. Several told me they wished they could have been introduced to this stuff at an earlier stage, that there could have been more of it.

We can, and should, be making this desire for broad, richly connected historical learning a priority.

* * *

In his latest book, *How to Educate a Citizen* (2020), E.D. Hirsch illustrates how easy it can be to impart knowledge without resorting to rote learning by quoting veteran teacher Dr. Michele Hudak:

> In my daughter's third-grade child-centred classroom, they were given a basic reader. Some of the stories are excerpts of classic literature and others are just stories that a publisher makes up . . . [But] you come to a knowledge-based

classroom, and the students begin their day with the Vikings. During reading we are exploring the Viking myths and having a rich discussion about that. We go to the domain-based read-alouds and we're now reading aloud about the Vikings. Everybody feels they're *getting* somewhere from one day to the next. And they are using sophisticated tier-three words in conversation . . .

[My kids] love it. They used to come home from school and we'd ask, "What did you learn today?" and they'd say "Nothing." And then once they got to a knowledge-centred school, we'd say, "What did you learn in history and geography?" And they talked and talked about it.[89]

The United States currently has two thousand core knowledge schools, including regular public schools, which focus on commonality and coherence of content, and their results are impressive. Schools in low-income neighbourhoods are smashing test scores, winning "Reward School" status and National Blue Ribbon Awards, and gaining incredible ground in both achievement and equity, proving Hirsch's point that "what a child is ready to learn largely depends on what she has *already* learned."[90]

Elsewhere, the benefits of a knowledge-rich foundation are also evident. In 2000, the Program for International Student Assessment (PISA) gave Germany scores in reading and math that were well below the international average. This prompted some major national soul-searching and ultimately led to the

German states cooperating to institute a shared-knowledge national elementary curriculum. (Let's pause there for a moment: Germany has sixteen federal states; Canada has ten provinces and three territories. And yet we're supposed to accept that nation-wide cooperation on something as important as school curriculum remains impossible in this country?) Following Germany's shift to a shared-knowledge curriculum, reading scores have steadily increased ever since, and Germany now ranks tenth in the world: up from twenty-second in 2000.[91]

Australia, for its part, has made history one of four mandatory pillars (the others being math, English, and science) nationally from K-12. Despite passionate political divisions on the subject (former Prime Minister John Howard was the first to relaunch the "history wars" by calling for more systematic teaching of the Australian story in 2006), all parties managed to agree on the importance of historical instruction, and the 2007 Labor government proceeded with the national history curriculum, with some modifications.

My own experience, attending elementary schools in three different countries, produced a variety and breadth of historical learning that undoubtedly shaped my passion for the subject. By the time I was eleven, I'd sat in a reconstructed bomb shelter, built a medieval castle out of sugar cubes, hammered my own version of an Aztec sun stone, written and illustrated a booklet on the Black Death, learned the history of the guillotine, and completed projects on Alexander Hamilton and the modern economy of Oman. I was lucky enough to attend an elementary school in Massachusetts where the principal was passionate about history and where the past was woven into the very fabric of school life, from the traditional Grade Four medieval assembly to the annual Roman Day chariot race (helmets and kneepads included).

At school in England, history was also a central part of primary years education. As seven-year-olds, we learned about the Second World War, with the main focus being the Blitz and the experiences of child evacuees. Today, the U.K. is currently in the midst of its own national reckoning with what history is taught, and how. Writing in the *Times Literary Supplement*, historian Frank Trentmann recently took aim at the *Life in the UK* handbook introduced by Boris Johnson's government; it's published by the Home Office and is required reading for anyone who takes a citizenship test. In the new version, Trentmann wrote, D-Day referred to "the British invasion of Europe" (with no mention of the Allies, although this has since been revised in the online version I found), while decolonization happened through "an orderly transition" with no mention of the violence of Partition or the emergencies in Kenya, Malaya, and Aden. Slavery is described as "an overseas industry" (this remains in the online edition) and Europe has been removed from an account of the Black Death, implying that it only affected Britain (ditto). There is also no mention of Hitler's racist ideology (still true of the online edition). Trentmann writes, "You do not need a PhD to know that Hitler was antisemitic or that people died in the Middle Passage. The earlier statement that the slave trade was 'evil' is no more complicated than the new preferred term 'booming.' Of course, history is complex, and the Holocaust certainly is. But that does not mean we cannot communicate it in a sensible manner . . . GCSE [high-school level] history includes the knowledge that Hitler held racist beliefs. Why should an official history for migrants not do the same?"[92]

The U.K. is also currently in the throes of its own debates about racial representation in academia, which histories to honour and include in school curricula, and which personalities are worthy of public monuments. But whatever disagreements continue to rage, the fact remains that in Britain, history is considered a subject *worthy* of national discussion and debate. And the Brits, of course, are spoilt with excellent historical TV programming hosted by authoritative presenters, which feeds into public engagement with the subject.

One example is the popular *Horrible Histories* series, which ran between 2009 and 2014 (you can still watch episodes online). Based on the books by Terry Deary, the series takes a Monty Pythonesque approach to history, featuring short comedic sketches and songs that riff on contemporary pop hits. During the pandemic lockdowns, our daughter developed a near obsession with the show, and many of the songs became the soundtrack to our lives for weeks and months at a time. Take Kylie Minogue's *I Should Be So Lucky* spin-off, set on a convict transport to Australia:

Those that lived were plucky, plucky, plucky, plucky
Crammed on board with rats and vermin, cockroaches in bed
Stench inside was sicky, yucky, yucky, icky
Lice not very nice, can't get them out of my head

Or Cleopatra's Lady Gaga-inspired ditty:

Married another brother, he's an okay geezer
But never told of my love for Julius Caesar
Had Caesar's child and hoped that he'd be crowned king
My bro said no, I said 'Oh!'—and I murdered him

Although there are segments on the Aztecs and the Greeks, the emphasis is mostly British, from Martha Howe-Douglas' tough, tattooed Boudicca—

My husband Presotagus died
He was a Celtic king
I was his queen, so due to me
Was half of everything

—to our family's favourite, a rap by Charles II (played by Matthew Baynton):

I love the people and the people love me
So much that they restored the English monarchy!
I'm part Scottish, French, Italian, and a little bit Dane
But one hundred percent party animal—champagne?

Has watching untold hours of *Horrible Histories* taught our daughter how to think like an historian? No. But it *has* taught her about the difference between the historical record and Shakespearean invention (while the jury's still out on the princes in the tower, Richard III probably didn't drown his brother in a vat of wine and never said "My kingdom for a horse!"); about the importance of recognizing Mary Seacole as well as Florence Nightingale; about religious and political hypocrisy in the trial of Joan of Arc; and about Darwin's theory of natural selection and why this upset the Christian establishment. We've learned plenty, too: I'd known enough about Caligula and Nero to tell her a bit about the excesses and crimes of certain Roman emperors, but I'd never heard of Elagabalus, who apparently fancied himself a bit of a practical joker (he catapulted venomous snakes at Roman theatre crowds and once surprised houseguests with a lion in their bed).

It's funny, weird, gross, catchy entertainment, and it's full of random facts. Is it a complete historical education? Certainly not. Is my kid hooked on history? Absolutely. And for now, that's a win.

* * *

This isn't at all to suggest that Canadian history instruction isn't without its own strengths. The breadth and variety of high school courses here is, I think, on balance preferable to too-early specialization (while as a first-year undergraduate I was awed by my peers' historical sophistication and expertise on certain subjects—subjects that, it turned out, they'd been studying for A-levels over the preceding two years in high school— I had a certain advantage in being able to relate events, periods, and places *beyond* "Hitler and the Henrys," as the most popular A-level history subjects are often described, because of the more generalist approach here).

And, of course, wonderful teaching happens in our public schools, too: one of the highlights of Grade Three for my daughter and her classmates was Pioneer Day, when their brilliant teacher assigned every child his or her own pioneer name and duties and the class followed a typical school day as it would have unfolded (with authentic packed lunches, historically accurate games and non-corporal punishments, and no electricity) circa 1850. (Interestingly, I'd note that there's plenty of direct instruction still happening in elementary French Immersion classes, perhaps because the challenges of mastering material in a second language means teachers have to cut to the chase a bit faster. This is not necessarily a bad thing.)

The Governor General's History Awards for Excellence in Teaching celebrate the very best of such creative and meaningful instruction. One example is 2019 recipient, Robert Bell, who enlivened his Grade Five/Six class's exploration of the Spanish Flu epidemic by leading his students to search for evidence about a child, Hazel Isabel Layden, who had attended their school and died in 1918 as a victim of the flu. Their research led them to local historians, museums and archives, and McMaster University, and even managed to connect with two of Hazel's living relatives who hadn't previously known one another, before culminating in a public exhibition.

Students whose curiosity is sparked, whose empathy is engaged, and whose capacity for understanding is honoured can grow up to be the ones making compassionate and informed political choices, adding to our shared knowledge, and sparking the imaginations of others. They may be the future historians being honoured by McGill's prestigious Cundill History Prize. They may be future Cundill Prize jurors. Or they may simply, but no less vitally, be the readers of the nominated titles. After all, stories need authors, but they also need readers. Without them, our stories, and our shared past, can easily vanish.

It's up to us to ensure that our past has a future.

The future of History

IN HIS MUCH-QUOTED graduation speech, Neil Postman distinguished between two ancient societies, those of the Athenians and the Visigoths, and their present-day manifestations:

> The first group lived about 2,500 years ago in the place which we now call Greece, in a city they called Athens. We do not know as much about their origins as we would like. But we do know a great deal about their accomplishments. They were, for example, the first people to develop a complete alphabet, and therefore they became the first truly literate population on earth. They invented the idea of political democracy, which they practiced with a vigor that puts us to shame. They invented what we call philosophy. And they also invented what we call logic and rhetoric.

They came very close to inventing what we call science, and one of them—Democritus by name—conceived of the atomic theory of matter 2,300 years before it occurred to any modern scientist. They composed and sang epic poems of unsurpassed beauty and insight. And they wrote and performed plays that, almost three millennia later, still have the power to make audiences laugh and weep. They even invented what, today, we call the Olympics, and among their values, none stood higher than that in all things one should strive for excellence. They believed in reason. They believed in beauty. They believed in moderation. And they invented the word and the idea which we know today as ecology.

About 2,000 years ago, the vitality of their culture declined and these people began to disappear. But not what they had created. Their imagination, art, politics, literature, and language spread all over the world so that, today, it is hardly possible to speak on any subject without repeating what some Athenian said on the matter 2,500 years ago.

The second group of people lived in the place we now call Germany, and flourished about 1,700 years ago. We call them the Visigoths, and you may remember that your sixth or seventh-grade teacher mentioned them. They were spectacularly good horsemen, which is about the only pleasant thing history can say of them. They were marauders—ruthless and brutal. Their language lacked subtlety and depth. Their art was crude and even grotesque. They swept down through Europe, destroying everything in their path, and they overran the Roman Empire. There was nothing a Visigoth liked better than to burn a book, desecrate a building, or smash a work of art. From the Visigoths, we have no poetry, no theater, no logic, no science, no humane politics.

Like the Athenians, the Visigoths also disappeared, but not before they had ushered in the period known as the Dark Ages. It took Europe almost a thousand years to recover from the Visigoths.

Now, the point I want to make is that the Athenians and the Visigoths still survive, and they do so through us and the ways in which we conduct our lives. All around us—in this hall, in this community, in our city—there are people whose way of looking at the world reflects the way of the Athenians, and there are people whose way is the way of the Visigoths. I do not mean, of course, that our modern-day Athenians roam abstractedly through the streets reciting poetry and philosophy, or that the modern-day Visigoths are killers. I mean that to be an Athenian or a Visigoth is to organize your life around a set of values. An Athenian is an idea. And a Visigoth is an idea.[93]

Individuals of an Athenian persuasion, Postman argued, value knowledge, art, public affairs, and historical continuity. By contrast, "Visigoths think of themselves as the center of the universe. Tradition exists for their own convenience . . . and history is merely what is in yesterday's newspaper."[94] Although Postman's descriptions may be historically simplistic, the metaphor is an instructive one for anyone interested in what a meaningful and complete education might entail.

Now, more than ever, historical knowledge matters. As Adam Chapnick wrote in November, 2020 in the *Literary Review of Canada*:

> In times of international strife, history is one of the most critical tools we have to remind us of the perils of ignorance. Sure, we must study the past to understand ourselves, but we must also think historically to better position ourselves to defend and preserve the broader liberal world order for which so many have sacrificed their lives and livelihoods . . . In twenty-first-century Canada, the fight for history is an existential one, and the forces of ignorance lined up against us are terrifying.[95]

The most obvious place to start is in our schools. In conversation with Steve Paikin on TVO's *The Agenda*, high school teacher Neil Orford cut straight to the chase:

> Let's make history compulsory . . . Let's make the argument that history needs to be broader in the curriculum. Let's make the argument that the liberal arts have been under assault by a math-science bias . . . If every high school has a pathway for math and science, there should be a pathway for history. And students should be pursuing that through

graduation. We will have better informed students and Canadians.[96]

The good news is that many people are coming to this realization already. If there's one thing that Donald Trump's presidency showed us, it's that while it's important to understand broad trends, niche histories, and how to challenge dominant narratives, at certain points in time it really does matter who's in power and how those individuals use that power. Knowing as many stories as possible from as wide a range of societies and cultures as possible can equip us to better appreciate and shape the systems that govern us.

These same systems are often the ones slowest to respond to calls for change. Provincial ministries of education (which are responsible for curriculum development) and school boards (which oversee the implementation of curriculum) are frequently at political loggerheads with educational departments, fuelling the ideological divide. The federal government is loath to enter the fray, owing to a discomfort around any suggestion that we instate a common history curriculum. And to it must fall to students, teachers, parents, and school communities to call to centre history as a subject in its own right, and to recognize that teaching history that is diverse and progressive shouldn't be mutually exclusive with teaching history that's purposeful and coherent. If we want the next generation to learn the history of their country as well as the full context of the world beyond our borders, we must demand change.

A national approach would be best. As Historica's Anthony Wilson-Smith remembers, the histories he was taught growing up in Montreal "were quite different than what was taught to my friends at the French-speaking school three blocks away. The best outcome would have been if we had each learned more about the perspective from the other side as well as our own. That should be a goal, but it's admittedly a very hard one to achieve." In the absence of a national movement, however, we can push the provinces to mandate at least three years of history in elementary school and three years in high school, as Granatstein has suggested.

"The solution now lies mainly with the public; opposition seems too entrenched among many of our education professionals," writes Hirsch. "The public needs to make the need for a common curriculum *more* threatening to the job of controversy-averse education officials than any conceivable gripe about a choice of particular content."[97] And an essential part of this lies in teacher training that truly supports and empowers teachers. "The first requirement for good teaching at every level is knowledge of the specific subject, not knowledge of pedagogical technique,"[98] Hirsch continues, in a statement that undoubtedly runs counter to what many curriculum specialists would argue (territorialism runs deep).

If we want students learning science from scientists and following a curriculum that has been shaped by scientists, we should want the same for students learning history. Let's not be ashamed to celebrate knowledge (indeed, in the months before he died of pancreatic cancer, beloved *Jeopardy!* host Alex Trebek himself mused on the value of knowledge: "I hope I've been an influence for good and an influence for the benefits of not minimizing the importance of knowledge in one's life," he said. "Even though you are not going to use a particular bit of knowledge, information that you acquire . . . becomes part of you and enriches you and makes you a better human being and I think a more understanding human being. The more you know, the easier it will be to understand everything else that's going on in the world. If you have limited knowledge, then you're approaching other people from a limited point of view, and that can be disastrous, as we have seen."[99])

Given the choice between a pedagogy specialist with a background in history or historian William Dalrymple (whose landmark *The Anarchy* describes in vivid and meticulously researched detail how the Mughal Empire came to be run by the East India Company, an organization based in a London office only five windows wide), I know who I'd rather have teach me about the rise of the world's first global corporate empire. This isn't to say that high school history teachers should be prize-winning historians, or that teachers shouldn't be trained in the latest pedagogical techniques, but that subject specialism matters.

A unified approach that recognizes the value and importance of a shared, diverse history, and commensurate support for teachers to deliver such a program, are the first of a brief list of recommendations I would make for those who hope to turn the proposals in this book into practical reality. This list would also include:

1. Nationwide and/or provincial commitment to centering national and global history in elementary and high school;
2. A commitment to diversification, as well as connection and continuity of taught histories;
3. Building bridges between the academy and schools, particularly in terms of textbook writing and teacher training;
4. Updated textbooks for schools that feature analytical, thesis-driven essays by professional historians at an accessible length (teachers have recommended the Major Problems series as one example).

While I believe in the importance of storytelling in the earliest years, as well as in a classical approach that allows students to circle back through topics and practise viewing historical moments through alternately wider and more focused lenses, all of the experts I've spoken with agree on the importance of any common curriculum not presenting history as a teleology, but rather as a contestable weaving together of stories with key moments selected to demonstrate the ways that interpretations of the past continue to change. "I like to see history as a great big messy enterprise," Margaret Macmillan told me. "It helps us formulate the questions, though it may not tell us the answers."

Although I wouldn't presume to propose detailed content, I would suggest that we would do students and our country a great service to widen our scope both temporally and geographically. All students should be entitled to an overview of world history that stretches from the Big Bang to Bitcoin, and that places Canada's history in a global context. Teaching global history is not easy, particularly given the wide range of different historical traditions and historiographies that must be taken into account; but "global literacy" (to borrow a term coined by veteran diplomat and author Richard Haas) is arguably the most pressing, and lacking, skill required for the next generation (students themselves appear to be on to this: world history is now more popular in the United States than European history, with more than twice as many students taking the former Advanced Placement exam). Canada's economy, Canada's climate, and Canada's vulnerability to a pandemic that respects no borders do not exist in a vacuum: in order to protect our national interests, it's vital that we understand the global forces at play.

Released in 2021, *The Dawn of Everything* by David Graeber and David Wengrow is a curious, playful, and ultimately hopeful approach to widening our understanding of human history and, specifically, social inequality. Anthropological, provocative, and anti-statist, it focuses on collisions between Indigenous and Western histories to offer an iconoclastic response to other "big" histories such as Harari's. Section headings include "How the conventional narrative of human history is not only wrong, but quite needlessly dull"; "In which we dispose of lingering assumptions that 'primitive' folk were somehow incapable of conscious reflection, and draw attention to the historical importance of eccentricity"; "On Woman, the scientist"; "In which we consider whether the Indus civilization was an example of caste before kingship"; and "Why the state has no origin." Readers may not share the authors' starting position or their conclusions, but the joyful conversation about history that it endorses is a welcome contribution. In addition to this, parents, teachers, and general interest readers might find any or all of the following titles useful as a first point of entry to some of the "big picture" questions around history:

E.H. Gombrich, *A Little History of the World*
Richard Haass, *The World: A Brief Introduction*
Lynn Hunt, *History: Why It Matters*
Neil MacGregor, *A History of the World in 100 Objects*
Margaret Macmillan, *The Uses and Abuses of History*
Sara Maza, *Thinking About History*

For younger readers:

Christopher Lloyd, *The Big History Timeline Wall-book*
Jo Nelson, *Historium: Welcome to the Museum*
Susan Wise Bauer, *The Story of the World*
Christophe Ylla-Somers, *All of Us: A Young People's History of the World*
The Dorling Kindersley History of the World
The Usborne Internet-Linked Encyclopedia of World History

And two excellent websites, with separate sections for teachers and students:

The Big History Project (https://www.bighistoryproject.com/home)
The World History Project (https://www.oerproject.com/World-History)

Canadians need to understand the differences between political traditions and histories in Canada and the U.S., as well as the political, legal, economic, social, and religious roots of these nations that are to be found in societies beyond our borders. In Robert Bothwell's words, "[Students] should learn that Canada is a middle-sized fish in a big pond and has always depended on allies and international institutions. Canada swims in an international ocean. We need absolutely to know about actions and precedents in the international system. We have to know what the system is and is not. If Canada comes to an end, it will be because of developments in the international sphere."

That said, international history needn't be threaded in only as it relates directly or obviously to us. When I asked hybrid teacher-coach Christina Ganev which key topics from world history every student should encounter before graduating, she replied, "Of course my mind goes to Columbus, the transatlantic slave trade, the Scientific Revolution and so forth, but what about early roots of democracy in India, or the Bantu settlement in sub-Saharan Africa (800 CE)?"

Indeed. The timing and placement of topics can, of course, be debated, as can the ways we interpret them, but we should embrace these discussions. As Lynn Hunt writes, debates over history's meanings "are a sign of [democracy's] health, not its weakness." Let's have those debates, and in so doing, let's prove that history really *does* matter. At the end of the day, Sam Wineburg notes, "When history is approached courageously and at its deepest levels, no new curriculum is needed to engage enduring questions of values. In classrooms like this, history cannot avoid issues of character."[100]

All the teachers I spoke with were optimistic about the future of history teaching and, indeed, the future of history itself. Students, too, "are generally hopeful in their disposition," Ganev observed. "History shows us that we can and do make progress. Studying the big-picture events helps students to feel hopeful, [while] teaching students to be active and engaged citizens is also another strategy to maintain hope and optimism for the future."

It's not too late for coherent, cumulative, substance-driven, broad, and inclusive history to be made a priority in Canadian schools. With enough pressure from parents, teachers, and students, all young people can know the joy and empowerment of a strong foundational understanding of our shared history. Perhaps most importantly, they can experience the wonder of the most human subject of all; a wonder captured by G.M. Trevelyan in his *Autobiography of an Historian:*

The poetry of history lies in the quasi-miraculous fact that once, on this earth, once, on this familiar spot of ground, walked other men and women, as actual as we are today, thinking their own thoughts, swayed by their own passions, but now all gone, one generation vanishing into another, gone as utterly as we ourselves shall shortly be gone, like ghosts at cockcrow.[101]

So what are we waiting for? The time to restore history to the centre of a meaningful education is now. Our future, as well as our past, may well depend on it.

Acknowledgements

M Y SINCERE THANKS TO all who took the time to share their experiences and expertise with me: Bob Bain, Graham Broad, Bob Bothwell, Rose Fine-Meyer, Christina Ganev, Perry Gauci, Lindsay Gibson, Bronwyn Graves, Natasha Henry, Danuta Kean, Margaret Macmillan, Tanya Maraj, Trish McMahon, Ruta Nimkar, Ken Osborne, and Anthony Wilson-Smith.

Thank you to Ken Whyte, for convincing me that an idea that wouldn't go away could be turned into a book and for his faith in my ability to write it.

And thank you, finally and always, to my family.

Appendix

OVER A PERIOD OF five months, I approached Ontario's ministry of education with several requests to speak to curriculum advisors on the following subjects:

- The reasoning behind an elementary/middle school history curriculum that leaps from first contact in Canada to ancient times, then back to modern Canada, then to the Middle Ages
- The omission of such subjects as the Holocaust (including from a Canadian perspective, e.g. of turning away the *MS St Louis*) from the Grade One to Eight curriculum, and how decisions are undertaken to weigh such topics against, for instance, residential school history (which is mentioned fifty times in the same document)
- The limitation of teaching history beyond Canada's borders to Grades Four and Nine

- The limitation of mandatory high school history to a single course in Grade Ten

The following is the response I received on Jan 18, 2021:

Dear Trilby Kent,

Thank you for your email regarding learning about Canadian history in Ontario's curriculum. I am pleased to respond.

You may be interested to know that in Ontario, the curriculum is regularly reviewed to ensure that the learning and skills being developed are coherent from Kindergarten to Grade Twelve and to maintain alignment with other curriculum-linked policies and priorities. Revisions are research-based and evidence-informed, beginning with benchmarking, or comparison, of Ontario's curriculum with those from across Canada and around the world.

Every curriculum revision involves extensive consultation with education stakeholders, as well as parents and students at key stages throughout the process. Writing of curriculum expectations is done by teams of educators, who are specialists in the subject area under review, and have experience teaching in Ontario's public education system.

Prior to release, a revised curriculum is reviewed by external experts. These reviewers have expertise in the subject area and are often selected from colleges, universities, subject associations, and/or professional organizations.

Their feedback helps ensure that the curriculum remains current, relevant, developmentally appropriate and reflects the needs and aspirations of diverse learners.

In regards to your query about residential school learning, in September 2018, schools across Ontario began the mandatory implementation of the revised elementary Social Studies Grades One-Six: History and Geography Grades Seven-Eight and the Canadian and World Studies, Grades Nine-Ten curricula. The revisions made learning about First Nation, Métis and Inuit perspectives, cultures, contributions, and histories, including topics of significance such as residential schools and treaties, a mandatory component of every student's education in Grades Four to Eight and Grade Ten. This work to revise the curriculum was done in collaboration with Indigenous and education partners.

Further, learning about human rights and genocide, including the Holocaust, is a mandatory component of the Grade Ten Canadian History Courses. For example, as part of the existing Grade Ten Canadian History since World War I (CHC2D) course, students will:

- Assess the significance of public acknowledgements and/or commemoration in Canada of past human tragedies and human rights violations, both domestic and international (e.g., *the Holocaust; the Holodomor; the Armenian, Rwandan, and Srebrenican genocides; the Chinese head tax; the Komagata Maru incident; Ukrainian and Japanese-Canadian internment; residential schools; the arrest of Viola Desmond; the demolition of Africville; forced relocation of Inuit families; suicide rates among Indigenous youth).*

Mandatory learning about human rights is also part of the compulsory Grade Ten Civics and Citizenship (CHV10) course. In this course, students explore the rights and responsibilities associated with being an active citizen in a democratic society and develop their understanding of the role of civic engagement, including exploring human rights violations, including examples about genocide, and assessing the effectiveness of responses. For example, students will:

- Identify examples of human rights violations around the world *(e.g., hate crimes, torture, genocide, political imprisonment, recruitment of child soldiers, gender-based violence and discrimination)*, and assess the effectiveness of responses to such violations *(e.g., media scrutiny; government sanctions; military intervention; regional, national, and/or international tribunals; boycotts; pressure from governments and/or NGOs)*.

With respect to your question about mandatory history credits at the secondary level, the Ontario Schools, Kindergarten to Grade Twelve: Policy and Program Requirements, 2016 document sets out the diploma requirements for earning an Ontario Secondary School Diploma (OSSD). The diploma requirements, including earning a minimum of thirty credits, are designed to ensure students are equipped with the skills and knowledge they need to succeed in their future pathway. As students enter secondary school and progress through to senior grades, they have more opportunities to select courses and programs that are of personal interest and those that can lead to their post-secondary destinations of choice, including apprenticeship, college, community living, university or the workplace. There are six history courses available in the Canadian and World Studies, Grades Eleven-Twelve curricula that have an international focus, and are offered for multiple pathways. Students can use these courses as a Group 1 credit for the OSSD.

All schools are directed to offer both a sufficient number of courses and courses of appropriate types to enable students to meet the diploma requirements. Please note that schools are not expected to offer all courses in all course types but must provide a range of choices appropriate to the needs and interests of their students.

Thank you again for writing. I hope this information is helpful.

Sincerely,

Original signed by
Mishaal Surti
Manager
Curriculum, Assessment and Student Success Policy Branch
Ministry of Education

Notes

1 Martin Gilbert, ed. *Churchill: The Power of Words – His Remarkable Life Recounted Through His Writings and Speeches* (Boston: Da Capo Press, 2012), p.423.

2 Anthony Seldon, "Why every government department needs a resident historian," *Prospect*, May 1, 2020.

3 Chimamanda Ngozi Adichie, "The Danger of a Single Story," TED, Oct. 7, 2009, YouTube video, 19:16, https://youtu.be/D9Ihs241zeg.

4 Harriet Sherwood, "Nearly two-thirds of US young adults unaware 6m Jews killed in the Holocaust," *Guardian* (Manchester), 16 Sept., 2020.

5 Joanna Lavoie, "TDSB must act now to stop anti-Semitism following incidents at an east-end school, says Jewish group," Feb., 22 2022.

6 Neil Postman, "My Graduation Speech," in *Conscientious Objections* (New York: Alfred A. Knopf, 1988).

7 Susan Wise Bauer, *The Well-Trained Mind: A Guide to Classical Education at Home* (New York: W.W. Norton & Co., 2009), p.106.

8 Richard Ovenden, *Burning the Books*, p.218

9 Ovenden, *Burning the Books: A History of Knowledge Under Attack* (London: John Murray, 2020), p.209.

10 Margaret Macmillan, *The Uses and Abuses of History* (Toronto: Penguin, 2009), p.128.

11 Daniel Immerwahr, "History Isn't Just for Patriots," *Washington Post*, Dec. 23, 2020.

12 *Ideas with Nahlah Ayed*, "True History in the Age of Fake News: The 2019 Cundill Panel," CBC Radio, Feb. 17, 2020.
13 Lynn Hunt, *History: Why It Matters* (Cambridge, U.K.: Polity Press, 2018), p.1.
14 *Ideas with Nahlah Ayed*, "True History in the Age of Fake News." *Ideas*.
15 Jo Guldi and David Armitage, *The History Manifesto* (Cambridge: Cambridge University Press, 2014), p.4.
16 Robert Fulford, "A review of Canada: A People's History on CBC-TV," *National Post*, Jan. 16, 2001.
17 Jordan Gill, "Repeating History: Some educators say New Brunswick curriculum is failing students," CBC News, July 4, 2021.
18 Steven Heighton, *Reaching Mithymna: Among the Volunteers and Refugees on Lesvos* (Windsor, Ont.: Biblioasis, 2020)
19 E.D. Hirsch, *How to Educate A Citizen: The Power of Shared Knowledge to Unify a Nation* (New York: Harper, 2020).
20 Marc-Andrew Ethier and David Lefrançois, "Learning and Teaching History in Quebec: Assessment, Context, Overlook," in *New Possibilities for the Past: Shaping History Education in Canada*, ed. Penney Clark (Vancouver: UBC Press, 2011), p.327.
21 Dorothy Williams, *Black in Montreal 1628-1986: An Urban Demography* (Montreal: Editions Yvon Blais, 2008), p.4.
22 Samantha Cutrara, "In Conversation with Natasha Henry (Pandemic Pedagogy Convo 26) Imagining a New 'We,'" June 9, 2020, YouTube video, 56:15, https://www.youtube.com/watch?v=cNZ1LSMS2CM.
23 Canadian Historical Association, "Canada Day Statement: The History of Violence Against Indigenous Peoples Fully Warrants the Use of the Word 'Genocide'," *Canadian Historical Association*, July 1, 2021. https://cha-shc.ca/news/.
24 "Historians Rally vs. 'Genocide' Myth," open letter, *Dorchester Review*, Aug. 12, 2021.
25 Michael Marker, "Teaching History from an Indigenous Perspective: Four Winding Paths up the Mountain," *New Possibilities for the Past:*

Shaping History Education in Canada, ed. Penney Clark (Vancouver: UBC Press, 2011), p.97-98.

26 Catharine Porter, "Schitt's Creek, Star, and His Fans, Are Taking Indigenous Studies," *New York Times*, Sept. 26, 2020.

27 Sierra D'Souza Butts, "Tipi raised at Ecole St. Lazare," *Toronto Star*, Nov. 27, 2021.

28 Susan Bell, "'Telling ourselves into the future': Quebec Cree finish rollout of new history curriculum," CBC News, Aug. 27, 2021.

29 Canadian Press, "Nunavut project to collect Inuit elder testimony on Franklin shipwreck sites," CBC News, Feb. 13, 2018.

30 Hunt, *History: Why It Matters*.

31 Macmillan, *The Uses and Abuses of History*, p.36.

32 Stewart, J.D.M., "History should be debated, not expunged," *Hub*, July 14, 2021.

33 Wineburg, *Historical Thinking and Other Unnatural Acts*, p.100.

34 Sam Wineburg, *Historical Thinking and Other Unnatural Acts*, p.17.

35 John Jeremiah Sullivan, "The Art of Non-fiction No. 11: Annette Gordon-Reed," *The Paris Review*, no. 238 (Winter 2021), p.145

36 "The Undoing of History," *The Agenda*, TVO, Jan. 8, 2020.

37 Conor Duffy, "University fees to be overhauled, some course costs to double as domestic student places boosted," ABC News (Australia), June 19, 2020.

38 Trilby Kent, "Unserious Ontario", *The Dorchester Review*, Spring-Summer 2018

39 Louise Brown, "Ontario lauded for high school history curriculum," *Toronto Star*, Jan. 23, 2016.

40 *The Ontario Curriculum: Social Studies, Grades 1-6; History & Geography, Grade 7-8.* (Toronto: Ontario, Ministry of Education, 2018), p.11.

41 See Appendix for a reply received in January 2021.

42 Bob Davis, *Whatever Happened to High School History? Burying the Political Memory of Youth, Ontario: 1945-1995* (Toronto: James Lorimer & Co., 1995), p.4.

43 Davis, *Whatever Happened to High School History?*, p.38.

44   Davis, *Whatever Happened to High School History?*, p.49.

45   Davis, *Whatever Happened to High School History?*, p.154.

46   Paul Bennett, *The State of the System* (Montreal and Kingston: McGill-Queen's University Press, 2020), p.180.

47   Davis, *Whatever Happened to High School History?*, p.41.

48   Davis, *Whatever Happened to High School History?*, p.78.

49   Davis, *Whatever Happened to High School History?*, p.74.

50   Granatstein, *Who Killed Canadian History?*, p.31.

51   Granatstein, *Who Killed Canadian History?*, p.33.

52   Granatstein, *Who Killed Canadian History?*, p.13.

53   Amy von Heyking, "Historical Thinking in Elementary Education: A Review of Research," in *New Possibilities for the Past: Shaping History Education in Canada*, ed. Penney Clark (Vancouver: UBC Press, 2011), p.179.

54   von Heyking, "Historical Thinking in Elementary Education," *New Possibilities for the Past: Shaping History Education in Canada* (Vancouver: UBC Press, 2011), p.185.

55   Keith C. Barton (@kcbarton), Twitter post, Oct. 21, 2020, 5:20 p.m., https://twitter.com/kcbarton/status/1319025781079670784.

56   Barton (@kcbarton), Twitter post, Oct. 21 2020, 6:43 p.m., https://twitter.com/kcbarton/status/1319046700095442944.

57   Diane Ravitch, "Tot Sociology: Or What Happened to History in the Grade Schools," American Scholar 56, no. 3 (Summer 1987), pp.343-54; reprint by National Council for History Education, History Matters, December 1996.

58   Bruce Frazee and Samuel Ayers, "Garbage In, Garbage Out: Expanding environments, constructivism, and content knowledge in social studies," Where Did Social Studies Go Wrong?, ed. James Leming, Lucien Ellington, and Kathleen Porter (Washington, D.C.: Thomas B. Fordham Foundation), p.112.

59   Susan Wise Bauer, *The Well-Trained Mind: A Guide to Classical Education at Home* (New York: W.W. Norton & Co., 2009), p.108.

60   Quebec Education Program (Approved Version), "Chapter 7: Social

Sciences – Elementary" (Quebec: Quebec Ministry of Education, 2001), p.186.

61 Graham Broad (@ProfessorBroad), Twitter post, Oct. 25, 2020, 7:05 a.m., https://twitter.com/ProfessorBroad/status/1320320539379044353.

62 Daniel T. Willingham and David B. Daniel, "Making Education Research Relevant: How researchers can give teachers more choices," *Education Next*, vol. 21, no. 2: pp.28–33.

63 "Teaching History in Ontario," *The Agenda*, TVO, Apr. 22, 2014.

64 Kristin Rushowy, "Ontario curriculum, textbooks outdated in many subject areas, auditor general finds," *Toronto Star*, Dec. 7, 2020.

65 Carla L. Peck, "Repulsive, Regressive and Racist: the 3Rs of Alberta Social Studies Under the UCP," blog post, Oct. 21, 2020, https://carlapeck.wordpress.com/2020/10/21/repulsive-regressive-and-racist-the-3rs-of-alberta-social-studies-under-the-ucp/.

66 Greg Ashman (@greg_ashman), Twitter post, 6:16 p.m., Apr. 19, 2021.

67 Daisy Christodoulou, *Seven Myths About Education* (Oxford: Routledge, 2014), p.67.

68 Peck, "Repulsive, Regressive and Racist.")

69 Sam Wineburg, *Why Learn History (When It's Already on Your Phone)?* (Chicago: University of Chicago Press, 2018), p.78.

70 "Core Convictions: An Interview with E.D. Hirsch," *New America*, Sept. 26, 2006, https://www.newamerica.org/education-policy/edcentral/core-convictions/.

71 Daniel T. Willingham, *Why Don't Students Like School? A Cognitive Scientist Answers Questions About How The Mind Works and What It Means for The Classroom* (San Francisco: John Wiley, 2009), p.21.

72 Bauer, The Well-Trained Mind, p.231.

73 Willingham, *Why Don't Students Like School?*, p.97.

74 Willingham, *Why Don't Students Like School?*, p.108.

75 Ruth Sandwell, "History Is a Verb: Teaching Historical Practice to Teacher Education Students," in *New Possibilities for the Past: Shaping*

History Education in Canada, ed. Penney Clark (Vancouver: UBC Press, 2011), p. 227.

76 Samantha Cutrara, "Updates: June 2020", blog post, https://www.samanthacutrara.com/updates.

77 Samantha Cutrara, "Thinking About History Curriculum in Canada (while also recognizing the informal curricula we carry)," ActiveHistory.ca, June 27, 2018.

78 Samantha Cutrara, "The Settler Grammar of Canadian History Curriculum: Why Historical Thinking Is Unable to Respond to the TRC's Calls to Action," *Canadian Journal of Education*, vol. 41, no. 1 (2018), https://journals.sfu.ca/cje/index.php/cje-rce/article/view/3156/2492.

79 Paul Bennett, *The State of the System* (Montreal and Kingston: McGill-Queen's University Press, 2020), p.232.

80 Robert Girvan, "RE: Historical Friction," Letters, *Literary Review of Canada*, June 2021.

81 Sam Wineburg, *Historical Thinking and Other Unnatural Acts: Charting the future of teaching the past* (Philadelphia: Temple University Press, 2001), p.6.

82 Wineburg, *Historical Thinking and Other Unnatural Acts*, p.24.

83 Lynn Hunt, *History: Why It Matters* (Cambridge: Polity Press, 2018), p.40.

84 Willingham, *Why Don't Students Like School?*, p.64.

85 Natalie Wexler, "Elementary Education Has Gone Terribly Wrong," *Atlantic*, August 2019.

86 Davis, *Whatever Happened to High School History?*, p.175.

87 Susan Wise Bauer, "On History, Children, and the Inevitability of Compromise," Comment, Sept. 4, 2014.

88 Peter Seixas and Penney Clark, "Obsolete Icons and the Teaching of History," in *New Possibilities for the Past: Shaping History Education in Canada*, ed. Penney Clark (Vancouver: UBC Press, 2011), p.297.

89 E.D. Hirsch, *How to Educate a Citizen* (New York: HarperCollins, 2020), p.48.

NOTES

90 Hirsch, *How to Educate a Citizen*, p.105.
91 Hirsch, *How to Educate a Citizen*, p.130.
92 Frank Trentmann, "How Not To Be An Alien," *Times Literary Supplement*, Sept. 4, 2020.
93 Neil Postman, "My Graduation Speech," in *Conscientious Objections* (New York: Alfred A. Knopf, 1988).
94 Postman, "My Graduation Speech."
95 Adam Chapnick, "Service Records: The Changing Ways We Remember," *Literary Review of Canada*, November 2020.
96 "Teaching History in Ontario," *The Agenda*, TVO, Apr. 22, 2014.
97 Hirsch, *How to Educate a Citizen*, p.155.
98 Hirsch, *How to Educate a Citizen*, p.174.
99 Amanda Bell, "Jeopardy! Host Alex Trebek Reflects on His Legacy: I Hope I've Been an Influence for Good," *TV Guide*, Jan. 8, 2020.
100 Wineburg, *Historical Thinking and Other Unnatural Acts*, p.230.
101 G.M. Trevelyan, "Autobiography of an Historian," *An Autobiography and Other Essays* (New York: Longmans, Green and Co., 1949).

Index

Note: Page numbers followed by 'n' refer to notes.

H
Haass, Richard, 161
Hamilton, Alexander, 141
Hammurabi, 135
Harari, Yuval Noah, 129, 160
Hatshepsut, 135
Heighton, Steven, 33, 172n18
Henry, Natasha, 38, 39
Henry VIII, 94, 135
Hirsch, E.D., 32, 33, 101, 104, 135,
139, 140, 157, 172n19, 178n88–
178n90, 178n96, 178n97
Hitler, Adolf, 46, 142, 143, 150
Howard, Catherine, 135
Howard, John, 141
Howe-Douglas, Martha, 146
Hudak, Michele, 139
Huggins, Nathan, 131
Hunt, Lynn, 23, 46, 80, 115, 161,
162, 172n13, 173n30, 177n82

I
Immerwahr, Daniel, 20, 172n11
Issa, Omayra, 36

J
Jacoby, Sanford, 25
Jesus, 90
Joan of Arc, 149

K
Kamookak, Louie, 45
Kean, Danuta, 165

Kelly, Christine, 78
King, Martin Luther, 62
King, Thomas, 42

L
Lawrence, T.E., 8, 74
Layden, Hazel Isabel, 150
Lecce, Stephen, 91
Lefrançois, David, 34
Lepore, Jill, 23
Levitt, Michael, 17
Levy, Dan, 44
Lincoln, Abraham, 47, 51
Lloyd, Christopher, 161
Louis XVI, 124, 137
Lovell, Julia, 24
l'Overture, Toussaint, 54
Lynes, Andrew, 88

M
MacDonald, John A., 48, 49
MacGregor, Neil, 161
Mackenzie, Alexander, 50
Macmillan, Ann, 95
Macmillan, Margaret, 20, 95,
114, 129, 159, 161, 172n10,
173n31
Mandela, Nelson, 62
Mao Zedong, 20
Marker, Michael, 42, 43
Marshall, H.E., 94
Matisse, Henri, 28
Maza, Sara, 161